The Empty Womb

by

Audrey Wyatt Shrive

The Empty Womb

Published April 2023 by Audrey Joy (Wyatt) Shrive

ISBN: 978-1-7362720-3-9

Contact the publisher and/or author at: ThisIsFromMe2020@gmail.com

Credits:

Cover Design, Layout, Editing by Alane Pearce, Professional Writing Services.
Cover Image from Unsplash.com

Interior design and layout by Alane Pearce, Professional Writing Services.

Publishing coaching, and project management by Alane Pearce, Professional Writing Services. Contact Alane at apearcewriting@gmail.com

Shrive, Audrey Joy Wyatt: The Empty Womb
1. Memoir 2. Christian Living 3. Infertility

Table of Contents

Chapter One
Children are a Gift from God

My Journey

The x-ray room was cold and dark. The only thing between me and the steel table I was lying on was a hospital gown. The TV monitors in the room were on so the ultrasound could capture what happened when the doctor pushed dye through my fallopian tubes. There were three men in the room with me; the doctor, the ultrasound tech and a male nurse to assist. There were no stirrups for me to rest my feet in for the procedure. I had to hold my legs up on my own. The doctor made the mistake of letting me see the needle which was now inserted between my legs and into my cervix. I swear that sucker was at least a foot long, maybe longer. And he wanted me to scoot my bottom closer to him. I refused. I was aware of the human anatomy and the basic size of a uterus.

"You're going to puncture my uterus with that needle!" I cried out.

"No, I won't," he answered.

"I'm not moving until you take that thing out of me," I responded.

"No, it's in already. I just need you to scoot closer to the end of the table. It will make it easier for me to do the dye injection," he explained. "Just an inch or so."

I'm not easily embarrassed or humiliated. This was an exception. These three men, had no understanding or compassion for what was happening to me and what they were asking me to do. I fought back the tears and did my best to comply with the 'bottom scoot', in a hospital gown, legs spread, and a gigantic needle in my cervix. After two or three false starts, I finally got in the position that would make the procedure easier for *him*. Nothing about this situation was easy for me.

Finally, he pushed the dye through my cervix. Only one fallopian tube showed free spill. The right one was partially blocked. My infertility issue was made more complicated.

The doctor was a general practitioner. He and his wife struggled to get pregnant. He treated her and they eventually were able to have children. Rather than refer me out to a specialist, he was determined to 'fix me'.

We were stationed at Ft. Bragg and he was an active-duty doctor at Womack Army hospital. Generally, I would say my healthcare from the military has been outstanding. Medical treatment by Dr. Know-It-All is the only negative experience

I've had in 30 years of military healthcare. My first meeting with him was actually my first appointment ever at a military hospital. I was a brand-new Army wife and brand new to military everything, including being seen at a military hospital. I don't know why it surprised me, but it did, when he walked in the room to do my annual pap and breast exam wearing BDU's (Battle Dress Uniform). Doctors wear scrubs and white coats, not "I'm-on-my-way-to-battle" attire. It just set me back a bit.

After the pap, which in and of itself has to be one of the most humiliating cancer screenings ever devised, he moved to the breast exam. This BDU wearing doctor/soldier said this to me as he did the exam:

"When you do your self-exam each month, think of the breast as a target and the nipple as the bull's eye. Work your way in from the outside of the target, into the bullseye, checking for any lumps or deformities."

I actually looked at his face to see if he was joking. He was not. Dr. Know-It-All was as serious as a heart attack. I wanted to laugh so badly, but it just seemed inappropriate to laugh while he had both hands on my breasts, doing the exam. He'd just seen my huha, now he was referring to my breasts as a target.

Once the exam was completed and I was dressed, he came back in the room. I told him then my husband and I had been trying to conceive for over a year and were having no luck. I also told him I didn't feel my cycles were regular and I was having break-through bleeding each month.

He basically told me to give it a little more time. And so, I did. Another year went by. We still weren't pregnant. A friend suggested I take my husband with me to the next appointment.

"Sometimes doctors take the wives more seriously if the soldier goes with you to the appointment," she said. It was the early 90's, so I suppose we hadn't come all that far. The military was certainly a man's world at that time.

I followed the advice. I warned my husband about the 'target' business and told him if he laughed he'd be in big trouble. We completed the pap and moved onto the breast exam. Right on cue Dr. Know-It-All said, "Think of the breast as a target….."

There was a great deal of snorting and coughing from the other side of the room to hide the laughter coming out of my husband's mouth. When we had our post exam meeting, he brought up the fact that we'd been trying for two years and were not getting pregnant. Thus began our infertility journey with Dr. Know-It-All.

God's Perspective on Children

> Behold, children are a gift of the Lord; The fruit of the womb is a reward. Like arrows in the hand of a warrior, so are the children of one's youth. How blessed is the man whose quiver is full of them; They shall not be ashamed when they speak with their enemies in the gate (Psalm 127:3-5 NASB).[1]

Opinions are like noses, everybody has one. There are a lot of well-meaning folks in the world who will give their two cents on any and all topics. Over the years I've learned the opinion that matters most is the Lord's. Isn't His opinion really the *only* one that matters? I've learned it's wise to examine what God and God's Word says on whatever subject is before me. Scripture has a lot to say on infertility. More than you might realize. My hope is to unpack some of those things on the pages of this book. Let's start with Psalm 127:3-5.

You may be surprised to know that Solomon wrote this Psalm. And these verses tell us four things:

- Children are a gift from the Lord.
- Children are a reward.
- Those who have children are blessed.
- Those who have children are not ashamed.

Let's start with the last one first. **Ashamed**. Scripture tells us in Jewish society before Christ, those who had no children believed they were being punished by God.[2] Why would they

---

1 All Scripture is from NASB, unless otherwise noted

2 Pg 146, The New Unger's Bible Dictionary

believe this? Well, first of all God gives the commandment to Adam and Eve to 'be fruitful and multiply' in Genesis 1:28. Right from the jump it's built into the human DNA to breed. It is a normal and natural desire to create a family, to bring children into the world.

Secondly, there was God's promise to Abraham that He would make him a great nation. God tells Abraham this three times. First in Genesis 12:2.

And I will make you a great nation, And I will bless you, and make your name great; And so you shall be a blessing.

Then in Genesis 13:16 God tells Abraham his descendants will be as the dust of the earth.

And I will make your descendants as the dust of the earth; so that if anyone can number the dust of the earth, then your descendants can also be numbered.

God promises Abraham a third time in Genesis 15:5.

And He took him outside and said, "Now look toward the heavens, and count the stars, if you are able to count them." And He said to him, "So shall your descendants be."

As a society, Israelites wanted to participate in the commandment to be fruitful and multiply and in making a really large nation. It follows, if they were as individuals unable to contribute to or participate in these two things, they would feel as if they were being punished by God for some reason.

We see several examples of this in scripture. In Genesis 30, for example, we learn that Rachel was barren. She watched her sister Leah getting pregnant practically by just looking at Jacob. After what must have seemed like eternity to Rachel, God turned the tables.

Then God remembered Rachel, and God gave heed to her and opened her womb. So she conceived and bore a son and said, *"God has taken away my reproach"* (Genesis 30:22-23).

Hannah's longing and desire for a baby in 1 Samuel chapter one is another great example of the desire to have children. Hannah's womb was closed. And, like Leah and Rachel, Hannah's husband Elkanah had two wives; Hannah and Peninnah. Scripture doesn't indicate they were sisters, but they had a similar situation as Rachel and Leah. Miss P was having all the babies and lorded it over Hannah, picking on her and irritating her. Hannah's heart was breaking and she poured out all of her pain and disappointment to the Lord in prayer. Hannah was ugly crying in the house of the Lord. It was so bad the priest thought she was drunk.

Hannah and Rachel were ashamed and broken hearted at their barrenness. Ashamed in this context means disappointed, delayed and to become dry. If you have walked this path, isn't this how it feels month after month to be disappointed? To start your menstrual cycle when you were so sure the fullness in your abdomen and the tenderness of your breasts was because you were finally pregnant? It's impossible really, to not be emotional and to not think you're being punished for something.

Psalm 127:5 also tells us you're **blessed** if you have children. In fact, the more the merrier. In Old Testament times it was very good to breed a small army. Not only did it take a lot of hands to do the work necessary to provide for the family, sons could help defend the family. It was as if they were weapons (arrows) to keep the family safe against enemies. As they grew older, they could also represent the family in civil cases that were resolved at the city gate. [3]

How blessed is the man whose quiver is full of them; They shall not be ashamed when they speak with their enemies in the gate (Psalm 127:5). This verse makes a lot more sense when you understand it in the context explained above.

Children, especially adult children, are an extension of their Father. Just like we're a type of extension of our Heavenly Father. As we walk through this earthly life, we represent Him. We are called to point people He puts in our path to Him.

Psalm 127:3 boldly states the fruit of the womb is a **reward**. This reward means payment of a contract. That makes sense in the context of the commandment to be fruitful and multiply, as well as God's covenant with Abraham. The 'reward' of having kids is God keeping his promise to the Jewish people and the people following the commandment to multiply. It also connotes benefits, compensation and wages. Sounds very cold, calculating and contractual. The implication could be interpreted as being performance based. Kind of like, "if I do my part God will do his."

What is 'my part' in today's world? As a believer in Jesus it would seem if one checks all of the boxes; prayer, time in the Word, serving, tithing, attending church regularly, it would be good enough to 'earn' a baby, wouldn't it? It seems like it worked out pretty regularly for the barren women of the Old Testament.

But, it's important to remember the covenant with Abraham was between God and the Israelites. We're under a new covenant now. Secondly, we live in a fallen world and circumstances

3 Pg 885, The Bible Knowledge Commentary

don't always work out the way we want them to. Our human bodies fail us sometimes. At the end of it all though, God is in control.

In the margin of my road weary Bible, I have written next to Psalm 127:3-5, "Why have I not received this reward?" It was written a full 8 years after I started trying to conceive. Like many women who have walked this road, I relate to Hannah and Rachel on a deep, deep level. If you've been down that weary path, you may as well.

Looking back to Psalm 127, verse 3 also tells us children are a **gift** of the Lord. In this instance children are a heritage of the Lord. A precious heirloom. An estate given to parents by God. God gives the best gifts. For the Israelite woman, a child, or many children, meant being a part of the commandment to be fruitful and multiply. It also meant they were contributing to the promise made to Abraham. But there was a third reason young Jewish women anticipated becoming pregnant.

The prophet Isaiah throws down quite the bombshell in the book of Isaiah.

Therefore the Lord Himself will give you a sign; Behold, a virgin will be with child and bear a son, and she will call His name Immanuel (Isaiah 7:14).

Isaiah not only prophesies the coming of the Messiah, but he also prophesies a virgin birth! This was taught to young women in Israel. They lived life with an expectation of His coming. And every young woman dared to hope that they may be the chosen virgin to bring the Messiah into the world.[4] If you think about it, Mary wasn't at all surprised by the concept of a virgin

4 Pg 146, The New Unger's Bible Dictionary

birth. She was surprised and humbled to be chosen. She really only had one question, "So tell me Gabriel, how's this going to work?" It's almost like she'd wondered about it before. Maybe many times. It's not hard to imagine Jewish teen girls chatting about the idea and wondering out loud just how God was going to pull that off.

So, what if the quiver is empty? What if there is no fruit of the womb? Does it mean God is withholding the gift? Does it mean God is withholding the reward? The blessing? Does it mean there is reason to be ashamed if there are no children?

For many women, becoming pregnant is not all glitter and unicorns. Experts tell us nearly 20% of women struggle with infertility. One in eight couples will struggle to conceive. There are a variety of factors that contribute to this; age, hormone issues, weight, abnormal cycles, anatomy issues in the uterus, ovaries or tubes. It's just not always that easy.

Looking back at Psalm 127, it's easy to overlook verse one. Those of us struggling to find answers to the empty quiver and wonder at the elusiveness of it all, may miss the most important part of the Psalm.

Unless the Lord builds the house, They labor in vain who build it. (Psalm 127:1).

The word build in this scripture literally means to build, but in a figurative sense, it means to obtain children. It is used in reference to having children. But not just having children, also having many descendants.[5]

Look at the blessing from the elders in Ruth.

---

5 Pg 187, Unger's Bible Dictionary

And all the people who were in the court, and the elders, said, "We are witnesses. May the Lord make the woman who is coming into your home like Rachel and Leah, both of whom *built the house* (italics added) of Israel; and may you achieve wealth in Ephrathah and become famous in Bethlehem." (Ruth 4:11).

Rachel and Leah are the mothers of the 12 tribes of Israel. Those women had many descendants. When building a house, someone must lay the first brick, drive the first nail, put up the first piece of lumber. It has to start somewhere and these two women (and their handmaidens), are the women who birthed the 12 boys who represented the 12 tribes that came into the promised land hundreds of years later. The elders, when blessing Ruth and Boaz had the benefit of hindsight to see how God had, and was, fulfilling his promise to Abraham.

But, unless the Lord builds the house, gives you arrows in your quiver, opens your womb, trying to become pregnant is vanity. It's useless. Believing you can control the outcome without God is false. It's a lie. It's a trap. And it's a trap I fell into in my quest to have children.

It's clear God is the source. Why, oh why, would He withhold the fruit, the reward, the blessed inheritance? Those are really big questions with no easy answers. I don't pretend to know the mind of God. I do see what he tells me in scripture. Let's unpack those truths together.

Read on dear reader. Read on.

If God doesn't build the house, the builders only build shacks. If God doesn't guard the city, the night watchman might as well nap. It's useless to rise early and go to bed late, and work your worried fingers to the bone. Don't you know he enjoys giving rest to those he loves?

Don't you see that children are God's best gift? The fruit of the womb his generous legacy? Like a warrior's fistful of arrows are the children of a vigorous youth. Oh, how blessed are you parents, with your quivers full of children! Your enemies don't stand a chance against you; you'll sweep them right off your doorstep (Psalm 127, The Message).

Chapter 2
The Closed Womb Has a Purpose

My Back Story

Before I was married, I moved to Colorado from Iowa. Even though I was on the pill, I started having breakthrough bleeding the month I moved. My doctor chalked it up to 'the change in altitude.' Okay, that was plausible I suppose. Additionally, I had a history of ovarian cysts. I knew this because those suckers would rupture from time to time. That is probably the most intense pain I have ever felt. The first time it happened, I thought I was going to die. I was at my boyfriend's and we were hanging out just watching TV. Next thing I knew, I'm on the floor on my hands and knees writhing in pain. I couldn't even speak to explain what was happening. I didn't really know what was happening! It stopped after about 10 minutes. For the next couple of days, my insides felt like a boxing match had taken place in my abdomen. I experienced this from time to time until I was well into my 40's.

When I described this to my doctor in Iowa, he said it was likely a ruptured cyst, but the only way to know for sure was if I could get to his office while the event was happening. Since these 'episodes' only lasted 15-30 minutes and his office was a minimum 2 hour wait, even with an appointment, I never bothered. He was correct in his diagnosis though, as an ultrasound confirmed the presence of ovarian cysts. I would have numerous ultrasounds over the years, when pain or discomfort would seem to indicate the presence of cysts. Each time the ultrasound would confirm what was suspected.

A few months after moving to Colorado, I went to my new OBGYN and told him I had a very large cyst on my right ovary. It was causing me a great deal of discomfort. Just the action of sitting down caused pain in my abdomen.

He countered it was impossible to have cysts, since I was on the pill. Post vaginal exam he apologized to me. "You have a cyst the size of a grapefruit. You know your body very well," he said.

A course of stronger birth control pills helped with the cyst and the breakthrough bleeding.

About a year after that, I got married and we started trying for a baby when we'd been married six months. I went off the pill. My menstrual cycle went off the rails. Every month I had spotting before and after my cycle. Some months I had bleeding all month long. I really, really relate to the woman with the blood issue in the Bible.

And a woman who had a hemorrhage for twelve years, and could not be healed by anyone, came up behind Him, and touched the fringe of His cloak; and immediately her hemorrhage stopped. And Jesus said, "Who is the one who touched me?" And while they were all denying it, Peter said, "Master, the multitudes are crowding and pressing upon you." But Jesus said, "Someone did touch Me, for I was aware that power had gone out of Me." And the woman saw that she had not escaped notice, she came trembling and fell down before Him, and declared in the presence of all the people the reason why she had touched Him, and how she had been immediately healed. And He said to her, "Daughter, your faith has made you well; go in peace" (Luke 8:43-48).

Mark 5:25-34 tells the same story, but gives us more details. She'd spent all she had trying to fix the problem. She'd endured much at the hands of doctors. They hadn't made her better. In fact, the opposite was true. She'd grown worse. Mark's version even tells us what she was thinking as she approached Jesus in the throng of people.

For she thought, "If I just touch His garments, I shall get well," (Mark 5:28).

And she did! She touched the hem of Jesus' garment and was immediately made well. What faith!!

It's a frustrating thing to know your body isn't working the way it's supposed to, no matter the health issue. But this woman!! Wow! Twelve years of constant menstrual flow. She would have been considered unclean. Everything she sat on or slept on or wore was considered unclean. Everything she touched and anyone who touched her would have also then been unclean, according to Leviticus 15:25-30. Technically, she was violating Jewish law just by being out in public.

Once she realized Jesus was on to her, she publicly explained why she touched Him! She admitted her issue literally in front of God and everybody. The courage and faith that took is mind-blowing. She had to be terrified of the response.

Jesus responds to her with great compassion. He calls her daughter. Because He knows even the number of hairs on her head, He knows the emotional pain she is in. He sees what this blood issue has done to her and he addresses her with a term of great endearment and tenderness. She fell asleep that night knowing she was healed and she was loved by Jesus.

My dysfunctional bleeding issue went on for several years, but not twelve. And while I don't live in a society that considered me unclean for my own blood issue, it felt unclean. It was unhealthy at worst, embarrassing and irritating at least. I also had months where I experienced very painful menstrual cycles. Not every month, but many months.

We moved from Colorado to North Carolina. My husband was a special operator at Ft. Bragg. By the time he and I had the conversation with Dr. Know-It-All, we'd been trying to get pregnant for two years and I'd been dealing with messed up cycles that entire time. Once we finally got Dr. Know-It-All's attention, he did his level best to help us. We started with the basics. The first and easiest test to do is to perform a sperm count on the dude. He passed with flying colors. He was not the issue. I was.

After the sperm test, the next step was to get lab work done on me and see where I had deficits. I don't remember what the results were, but I do remember I was put on Clomid for several months. Clomid is a medication that stimulates an increase in the amount of hormones that support ovulation. As long as I was on Clomid, my cycles were normal.

At the same time, I began using a Basil Body Temperature chart. If you've walked this path, you know the drill. Every morning, before getting out of bed, you take your temperature and note the reading on the chart. In theory, a woman's body temperature rises a degree or so when they ovulate. The chart also keeps track of your menstrual cycle and when 'coitus' occurred. That official medical term sounds as cold and calculating as trying to plan sex around ovulation feels.

Planning for this was made even more challenging as my husband's job in the Army called for him to train 300 out of 365 days. There were schools where he'd be away weeks at a time, trainings 'down range'(on Ft. Bragg, but not coming home at night), airborne operations and a myriad of other responsibilities. Oh, and the 65 days he was home wasn't exactly consecutive. A day here, a week there. His time and training were based on the needs of the Army. The Army didn't give a rip about my biological clock or my desire to have a baby.

It was made more emotionally challenging by the fact that literally everyone around us was having babies. Military folks are of childbearing years; 18 to mid-40's. Couples get pregnant and have babies in the military on a pretty regular basis. There's often a 'baby boom' 9 months after a deployed unit returns. I rejoiced with them and was happy for my friends. Until I wasn't.

We had been going down this path for what seemed like forever when yet another couple in our Bible study small group announced they were expecting. For the first time, I felt actual jealousy. This is a foreign emotion to me. I'm just not really a jealous person. But I recognized that ugly emotion for what it was. I smiled a fake smile and told them congratulations, but really, I was not happy. She was getting what I wanted.

On the drive home that night, my husband said somewhat jokingly, "I know why we're not getting pregnant. Other people are hogging them all!"

We both chuckled. It was just what I needed to snap me out of that negative path I almost headed down.

For two years I charted, got regular bloodwork, took meds, got ultrasounds and of course the horrible test described in chapter one. Nothing. Nada. Not even a hint of hope crossed my path.

And then, after four years of trying to get pregnant, my husband cheated and left.

When God Closes a Womb, There's a Purpose

And Sarai was barren; she had no child (Genesis 11:30).

Let's talk about Sarah and Abraham. They are introduced to us in Genesis 11. Abraham's Dad was named Terah. Terah had three sons Abraham, Nahor and Haran. Haran was Lot's Dad. They were living in Ur, where Terah was born. Haran died. Nahor married Haran's daughter and Abraham married Sarah. We get that as an introduction and then before the story goes on, verse 30 tells us all we need to know about Sarah. She was barren. A whole verse dedicated to this announcement. It's important.

The story of this family continues over the next several chapters. Terah, maybe looking for a fresh start after the death of his son, takes the family and leaves Ur. The members of the family that went were Terah, Abraham his son, Sarah his daughter-in-law, and Lot, his grandson. Nahor stayed behind. They travelled into Canaan and went as far as Heran. Terah died there at the ripe old age of 205 years!

In chapter 12, God starts talking to Abraham and makes His first promise to him. God tells Abraham to continue the journey, go farther into Canaan and God will make him a great nation. Verse 3 holds the biggest promise.

And in you all the families of the earth shall be blessed (Gen. 12:3b).

This second promise is the promise from God to make a way of salvation for the whole world, in Jesus the Messiah. God also promises Abraham in verse 7 that He will give the land of Canaan to Abraham and his descendants. Because there was a famine in Canaan, they continued the journey into Egypt.

Before they got to Egypt, Abraham and Sarah had a little chat. Since Sarah was beautiful, he was worried they would kill him to have her, so he told her to tell the Egyptians she was his sister. As expected, Pharoah liked what he saw and took Sarah into his house. He treated Abraham really well. He gave him sheep, oxen, donkeys, and camels. But God was not happy. Abraham put his wife in a compromising situation and asked her to be complicit with him in deceit. He put the purity of their marriage at risk and the promise God made to Abraham was also in jeopardy. The worst of it though, was Abraham didn't trust God to protect him! He took matters into his own hands. That never goes well.

God brought plagues on Pharoah's house. The Egyptians were a superstitious bunch. So, when the plagues came, Pharoah figured out what was going on. He kicked them out of Egypt. But Abraham got to keep all the loot! He became a very wealthy man due to his deception.

Once again, in chapter 13, God promises Abraham all of Canaan will be his and his descendants. God tells him his descendants will be as plentiful as there is dust on the earth.

Chapter 15 opens with God making a fifth promise to Abraham.

Do not fear Abraham, I am a shield to you; Your reward will be very great (Gen. 15:1).

Abraham asks God just what exactly is He going to give him. He reminds God he doesn't have an heir and the way things were going all he owned was going to go to a guy named Eliezer of Damascus. Eliezer was one of Abraham's household servants. But

God assures him he will have an heir and tells him to look at the stars. Count them if you can! This is how your descendants will be. Later in Chapter 15, God again promises Abraham his descendants will have the land of Canaan.

In the meantime, Sarah gets really tired of waiting for God to give her a child and decides to take matters into her own hands. She suggests Abraham have sex with her maid, Hagar. Maybe she could get a child that way. Abraham seems a little too eager to take his wife up on that suggestion. It was culturally normal, but come on Abraham! Sure enough, Hagar gets pregnant and they name him Ishmael.

In Chapter 17, we see God and Abraham having another talk. This is where God makes promise number six. Abraham is 99 years old. Old Abe begins making suggestions to God that it would be a lot easier if God would fulfill His promises through Ishmael. Nope. God tells Abraham in verse 15 of this chapter that Sarah will have a son and she will be the mother of nations; kings of peoples shall come from her. Abraham literally fell on his face and laughed. Not only was he 99, but Sarah was 90! She was so far past menopause even hot flashes were a thing of the past for her! But no, God insists this time next year, Sarah will have a baby. In chapter 18, God tells Abraham the same thing again and Sarah hears it. She gets a good chuckle too. The timing of this baby's birth is promise number seven.

Chapter 20 finds Sarah and Abraham on the move again. They journey to a land called Gerar. Abraham tells Sarah to tell them she's his sister. Stop me if you've heard this one before. Sure enough, the king of Gerar took Sarah into his home. His name was Abimelech. God came to Abimelech in a dream and told him that he was dead for taking a married woman into his home. Abimelech hadn't touched Sarah, so God said He would spare him if he would restore Sarah back to Abraham. God also tells Abimelech that Abraham is a prophet and Abraham will pray for him.

Abimelech wasted no time. As soon as he awoke, he told his servants what was going on. This scared them to death. He brought Abraham in and asked for an explanation. Abimelech got one. Abraham told him he was afraid for his life and so he told the 'white lie'. Sarah was the daughter of his father, but not his mother, so she 'really was his sister'. Each commentary I read had a different explanation for this weirdness. I concluded it doesn't really matter. God had blessed their marriage and given Abraham a great promise that would come through Sarah.

Even though he really hadn't done anything wrong, Abimelech gave Abraham sheep, oxen and servants as restitution. He also gave Him 1000 pieces of silver. He restored Sarah back to Abraham and he told Abraham to wander wherever he wanted in the land. He also gave them both a pretty good tongue lashing, then sent them on their way. But not before Abraham prayed for Abimelech and his household.

And Abraham prayed to God; and God healed Abimelech and his wife and his maids, so that they bore children. For the Lord had closed fast all the wombs of the household of Abimelech because of Sarah, Abraham's wife (Gen. 20:17-18).

Did you catch that? The women of this household were barren in the time that Sarah and Abraham were running their con. Their closed wombs didn't even have anything to do with them. Those women were guilty of no wrongdoing, yet God chose to close their wombs during the time the deception was happening.

I love that the heroes of the Bible are flawed people. It makes them more relatable. It gives me hope. They fail. A lot. Abraham lied. Abraham chose his own skin over protecting and honoring his wife. He did it not once, but twice. God made these amazing promises to Abraham and he just about screws it up by putting his wife in a situation that could have stolen Sarah's purity.

The *'Bible Knowledge Commentary'* has this to say on Chapter 20.

"This story records God's providential protection of His people, but it's emphasis is on purity, specifically the preservation of Sarah's purity. For the fulfillment of the promise, marriage is important; participation in God's promised blessings demands separation from worldly corruption.

Sinfulness and weakness of faith created a threat to the promised blessing. It is a sad commentary on one's lack of faith if God has to deliver him again and again."[6]

And in a later passage, "God made Abraham and Sarah one so that they might produce a godly seed. This was basic to the covenant.

Both deliverances of the patriarch preserved the purity of Sarah and kept the promise intact. The first incident (Gen. 12) however, was outside the Promised Land and reflected more clearly the life-and-death struggle of the nation in Egypt as God would later save them and deliver them. The second incident (chap. 20) was in the land and was an event in which God protected their marriage and thereby His promise. God controls birth; He mirac-

6 Pg 61, Bible Knowledge Commentary

ulously intervenes; He opens and closes wombs (vs. 17-18). No mere human potentate can thwart God's plan."[7]

God protected Sarah. He kept her pure. He kept her from committing adultery and destroying her marriage. God also protected Abraham. And Abimelech. And His promise to Abraham, which really was a promise to the world because Jesus was going to come through this promise to save the world from its sin. But that's another story for another day.

God closed Sarah's womb for a very, very long time. We'll circle back around to her a little later in the book. In this story though, God closed the wombs of every woman in Abimelech's household because of Abraham's sin and deception. In God's infinite wisdom, which is so far beyond ours, he just shut down all the baby-making until Abraham and Sarah could get themselves squared away. It was what was best for everyone at the time.

As for me, turns out, during our entire four-year marriage there were numerous 'drunken indiscretions' on the part of my husband. God knew there was deception. He knew I had no business having a child with this man. God knew the marriage would fall apart. So, in the height of the best childbearing years, He closed my womb.

I don't mean to imply that God only closes a womb when there is sin present. There are any number of reasons why God makes that choice. Some we may know this side of heaven, some we may never know in this life. Scripture tells us though, beyond any shadow of a doubt, when God closes a womb there's a purpose.

---

7 Pg 62, Bible Knowledge Commentary

Chapter 3
The Open Womb Has a Purpose

My 'Now What?'

When my very short marriage fell apart, I left North Carolina and moved back to Colorado. It seemed fitting to pick up the pieces closer to family and back in a place that was familiar. I had many friends in Colorado Springs and quickly reconnected. My physical issues continued. Cysts. Ruptured cysts, irregular cycles and break through bleeding. I once again sought medical help. The doctor suggested a D&C. Typically, this procedure is reserved for a situation where a miscarriage has occurred. My doctor said this was needed to clean my uterus out and give me a 'jump start' so to speak. Think of it like a computer re-set. And it worked! It was refreshing after so many years of 'dysfunctional bleeding', the official medical term, to have normal cycles!

I was back in Colorado about a year when I met a guy. He was also in the Army and had started his military career as an Airborne Ranger. He did a different job in the Army when I met him, but once you're a Ranger, you're always a Ranger. We dated for a year and a half. After my last wreck, I was cautious to move into anything too quickly. We got married and right away started trying for a family. He had two kids from his first marriage but agreed to try for a third with me. I was 36 when we started trying to get pregnant. We had no luck, so after about a year, we also sought help.

As before, the first step we took was to test his sperm. We were working with a gynecologist at Evans Army hospital on Ft. Carson. When we went to get the results, the doctor assured us my husband was not the problem.

"You have high mobility, strong swimmers and a sperm count of 87 million. You have Ranger sperm," the doctor proclaimed with a smile!

Never bashful and quite proud of the description, my husband told anyone who asked, and many that didn't, he had, 'Ranger Sperm!'

This same doctor performed an exploratory surgery on me. It was done laparoscopically and was a same day surgery. He wanted to get a look at things on the inside. It was noted that I had some endometriosis, (tissue that should be inside the uterus on the outside) but it was minor. I learned from doctors over the years, there is something about the presence of endometriosis that inhibits or prevents pregnancy. I also learned I have a tilted uterus. This just makes it harder for sperm to actually get into the cervix. So that's a problem.

After about a year of working with this doctor, he referred us to an infertility specialist in Denver. Of course, the first thing he did was run tests. Sperm test. Check. Still Ranger sperm with 91 million swimming. Lab work on me. Repeat the laparoscopic exploratory surgery, during which he also checked my fallopian tubes again. Thank goodness I was under anesthesia for that one. He reported good flow from both sides, so it made me wonder what Dr. Know-It-All had done wrong. That was really the only good news. Still had minor endometriosis. Still had a tilted uterus. And I was in my late thirties. My biological clock was ticking so loud it was deafening.

It took a few months to get all of the tests done and appointments made in Denver. We finally met with the doctor to get his recommendation as to how to move forward. It was in the fall of the year. His recommendation was we move forward with IUI (Intrauterine insemination). That's what it's called for humans. I grew up on a farm and ranch in South Dakota. This procedure, when done on cattle is called AI (Artificial Insemination). Now, that's a lot shorter and easier to say, (and type), so I'll be calling it that from here forward.

We agreed with his recommendation. I went back on Clomid and started charting my temperature again. And we scheduled our first AI.

The big day arrived. Our work schedules made it so we couldn't go together. The Ranger went and did his part. I arrived a couple hours later for the turkey baster procedure. The tech came in with a vile of sperm that had my husband's name on it. He indicated there were 1.3 million sperm.

Wait. What?!

"That's NOT my husband's sperm," I said with panic in my voice. "He has Ranger Sperm!"

The tech looked at me like I was slightly crazy. I went on to explain why I said what I said and told him in no uncertain terms, "You're not putting that in me, that's someone else's sperm!"

She patiently walked me through the entire process of how they protected the samples of each patient. They had many checks and balances in place intended to prevent mix ups from occurring and repeatedly assured me this was indeed my husband's sperm. I finally relented and the procedure went forward. The other thing I remember about the procedure is my uterus was so tilted that even the doctor had a hard time getting the sperm in the cervix. I remember thinking, 'No wonder I've never been pregnant. My very anatomy is preventing it.'

We did five rounds of AI. November, December of that year and then January, February and April of the following year. No luck. When we went in for the follow up appointment in April, the doctor suggested we move on to more drastic measures.

When God Opens a Womb, There's A Purpose

> Now the Lord saw that Leah was unloved and He opened her womb, but Rachel was barren (Gen. 29:31).

We meet Jacob in Genesis 25. He and his twin brother, Esau, are the grandsons of Abraham. The boys grew up and when they were young men, Jacob, who was the younger twin, stole Esau's blessing from him by tricking his old and blind father into thinking he was Esau. Earlier, Esau had sold his birthright to Jacob for a bowl of stew. The birthright went to the first-born male. Esau was the first twin born. The birthright meant getting a double portion of the Father's estate. Esau treated this important right with disdain and disregard. (Genesis 25:31-32)

Getting a blessing from the father was a high honor. Losing it was a blow. Blessings were usually encouraging, sometimes prophetic and may include information on the sons inheritance. We see Jacob's blessing, the one intended for Esau, in Genesis 27.

So he came close and kissed him; and when he smelled the smell of his garments he blessed him and said, "See, the smell of my son is like the smell of a field which the Lord has blessed; Now may God give you of the dew of heaven, and of the fatness of the earth, and an abundance of grain and new wine; May peoples serve you, and nations bow down to you; Be master of your brothers, and may your mother's sons bow down to you. Cursed be those who curse you, and blessed be those who bless you" (Gen 27:27-29).

Jacob now held all of the power cards. As you can imagine, Esau was more than a little angry and he vowed to kill Jacob once his father was dead. Rebekkah, their mother, caught wind of the plan and sent her son Jacob off to the land of Haran where her brother Laban lived. She was not only trying to spare his life, but she wanted him to marry an Israelite and not one of the 'locals' as Esau had.

Jacob went on the journey to his uncle's home. Uncle Laban took him in and also hired Jacob to work for him. Laban had two daughters; Leah, the older daughter and Rachel the younger. Jacob loved Rachel. We only know a few things about the sisters from scripture. Genesis 29 tells us that Rachel was a shepherdess and she was beautiful. The job of a shepherdess was physically demanding. It's likely that Rachel was both physically and emotionally strong. She would have been outside all day in the elements, bringing the sheep in at night, getting them to water and potentially even protecting them from wild animals.

Genesis 29 tells us the Leah was 'tender-eyed'. Some versions of the Bible say Leah's eyes were weak. This doesn't mean she couldn't see. The meaning of the phrase is that she was soft-hearted or tender-hearted. It's likely that Leah was very kind and caring. Probably didn't have the stomach for killing a predator as Rachel may have done to protect the sheep.

Jacob asks Laban for Rachel's hand in marriage and promises to work for his uncle seven years to earn the right to marry Rachel. Laban agrees to the terms. When the seven years were up, Laban pulls a fast one on Jacob and presents Leah as his bride. Jacob realizes this the morning after the wedding. The deceiver has become the deceived. Furious, Jacob confronts Laban.

A week later, Laban gave Rachel to him, but he has to agree to work for Laban for another 7 years. In the marriage agreements, Laban gave his maid Zilpah to Leah as her maid and gave Bilhah to Rachel as her maid.

Then the babies started coming. Though Rachel's womb was closed, Leah was bearing children right and left. Jacob might have loved Rachel more, but it seems he didn't mind having sex with Leah. Jacob's first born was **Rueben**. Leah named him this and it means *the Lord has seen my affliction*. Affliction here means depression, misery and trouble. Genesis 29:32b says, "Surely now my husband will love me."

Baby number two was **Simeon**. This means *the Lord has heard I'm unloved*. Then came **Levi**. Genesis 29:34b says, "Now this time my husband will become attached to me, because I have borne him three sons." Attached in this context means *to unite, abide with, cleave*.

Judah, meaning *praise*, was baby number four. By now, Leah has resigned herself to her plight and simply says, "This time I will praise the Lord" (Gen. 29:35).

Then the babies stopped for a while.

Leah was Jacob's first wife. She bore him six sons and he never treated her with the honor this position deserves. The word unloved indicates Jacob was indifferent to Leah. He neglected her needs and didn't elevate her as he should have. It's clear from these verses this wounded Leah and she knew it was wrong. I suspect she even loved him! Oh, the unrequited love that goes unnoticed is so tragic. Jacob had been there seven years already when good 'ole Dad put Leah in this impossible position. It's really not a stretch to think that she loved him and went along with Laban's plan, thinking she could win Jacob over in time.

By now, Rachel is fit to be tied. We see in Genesis 30:1-4, Rachel gets jealous and she blames Jacob for not getting her pregnant. Jacob becomes angry with her asking, "Am I in the place of God, who has withheld from you the fruit of the womb?" (Gen. 30:2b).

Then, in anger, Rachel gives her maid Bilhah to Jacob as a wife so Rachel can have children through her. (Sound familiar?) The plan works and a son named **Dan** is born. Rachel names him this saying, "*The Lord has vindicated me.*" The context here is *contend or strive*. Though Rachel has a son, she had to go to extra-ordinary measures to get this son. She was trying to control the uncontrollable.

Bilhah bears a second son named **Naphtali**. Leah says of this baby, *"She has wrestled with her sister and prevailed."*

Did she though? While Leah shows a lot of faith in God through her plight of being unloved, Rachel lacked faith. She didn't wait on God. She took matters into her own hands with the emotions of jealousy, anger and a belittling attitude toward her husband. The couple quarrels. While it was the cultural norm of the day, it almost makes one wonder if Jacob slept with Bilhah to get back at Rachel for her hurtful words.

I've always thought of Leah as being a bit of a trouble-maker, in cahoots with her dad to pull a fast one on her sister and Jacob. Scripture shows the opposite. Leah was the kind, loving and caring sister. She gave it her all as a wife and Jacob wasn't having it. The scriptures bear out that Rachel was the harder of the two sisters. It would explain why Jacob was attracted to her; she was a scrapper and so was he.

At this point, Leah realizes she's not having any more babies. So she gave her maid, Zilpah, to Jacob as a wife. Zilpah bears **Gad**, to which Leah declared, *"How fortunate,"* and with the birth of **Asher** Leah declares, *"Happy am I."* Her attitude has changed and is very different from her sisters.

Leah bore Jacob two more sons after this; **Issachar**, meaning *his reward would come*, and **Zebulun,** meaning *dwell with honor*. With the birth of son number six, Leah was still hopeful that her husband would *"Dwell with her since she had given him six sons."* (Gen. 30:20). Her faith was still strong. She was unloved, by her husband but had accepted her situation. She was full of gratitude because she knew God loved her.

Finally, in Genesis 30 we read this:

Then God remembered Rachel, and God gave heed to her and opened her womb. So she conceived and bore a son and said, *"God has taken away my reproach."* And she named him **Joseph** saying, *"May the Lord give me another son"* (Gen. 30:22-23).

So, at long last, Rachel had a son. This son was long-awaited and loved by both of his parents. As the scriptures go on, we learn he was Jacob's favorite and this caused a lot of jealousy on the part of his older brothers.

After 20 years, God tells Jacob to return to his home. He and Laban weren't getting along all that well anymore. Jacob had been much more prosperous in his business endeavors than Laban had. Laban was jealous. Jacob, Rachel, Leah and their entire entourage fled without a word to Laban and had been gone three days before he realized it. Laban went after Jacob and caught up to him. They had quite the showdown, but eventually hugged it out and Jacob went off with Laban's blessing.

Jacob was a little more than worried about returning home. Esau was in a mood to kill him when he'd left 20 years before. During the journey, Jacob cried out to God and prayed for deliverance from the hand of his brother. He reminded God on his journey away from home 20 years before, God promised Jacob that He would prosper Jacob and make his descendants as many as the sand of the sea. (Genesis 28:12-22) In Genesis 32, the night before he will see Esau again, Jacob sends all of his family, livestock and belongings ahead. He is left alone.

This passage tells us a man wrestled with him until daybreak. Likely an Old Testament appearance of Christ, Jacob wrestles with this man and refuses to let go until He blessed Jacob. God changes Jacob's name to Israel, saying this in verse 28:

"Your name shall no longer be Jacob, but Israel; for you have striven with God and with men and have prevailed" (Gen. 32:28b).

Yep, Jacob was a scrapper.

The next thing Jacob knew, Esau was barreling right down on him with 400 men. Esau ran to meet him, embraced him, kissed him and both men wept. Jacob introduces his family. Both brothers have been blessed by God and have become very successful. All is forgiven and they part ways with the break in their relationship repaired.

Jacob and company camped outside of Shechem in Canaan for a time. Then God told them to travel to Bethel. Jacob built an altar for God here. God appeared to Jacob and He blessed him.

God also said to him, "I am God Almighty; Be fruitful and multiply; A nation and a company of nations shall come from you, And kings shall come forth from you. And the land which I gave to Abraham and Isaac, I will give it to you, And I will give the land to your descendants after you" (Gen. 35:10-12).

They departed Bethel and set off for Ephrath. Along the way, Rachel went into labor. This little verse is just slipped in like it's no big deal. All this traveling around the country and Rachael is pregnant again! As they are traveling from Bethel to Ephrath, she went in to 'severe labor'. They're out in the middle of no-where and she's in trouble. The mid-wife assured her she would have another son. Her prayer for another son is granted with the birth of **Benjamin**. But, the labor was so severe she died in childbirth. Jacob buried her there. (Gen. 35:16-20) The wife Jacob loved was gone.

We're not told in scripture of any difficulty in labor with the birth of Joseph. It begs the question though, was Racheal's womb closed because more pregnancies would have ended her life sooner? She was physically strong. She was emotionally strong. But perhaps there was something in her anatomy that was not built for bearing the many children Leah did. Scripture doesn't tell us. We can only surmise. Perhaps that was one of God's purposes in closing her womb.

That said, God opened the womb of Rachael to give birth to Benjamin. Little Ben gave us the last piece of the puzzle to fulfill the need for the twelve tribes of Israel! So there they are in all of their glory; **Rueben, Simeon, Levi** (the Levites would be the spiritual leaders of Israel), **Judah** (Christ's genealogy line came through him), **Dan, Naphtali, Gad, Asher, Issachar, Zebulon,**

Joseph (who would save God's chosen people from starvation after his brothers sold him into slavery) and **Benjamin**.

God's purpose in opening the wombs of these women, when he did, gave us the foundations of the nation of Israel. The twelve tribes of Israel came through Jacob and his wives.

When God opens a womb, there's a purpose.

Chapter 4
When a Womb is Open, Often Someone Prayed

My Prayers

I had reached a difficult crossroads in my quest to have a baby. There was the mystery of my husband's suddenly low sperm count. And I had old eggs. I was 39 years old and had never been pregnant. The infertility doctor told us our best course of action was to use another woman's eggs and my husband's sperm to create twelve to fifteen embryos. In this process, normally what happens is multiple embryos are transferred to the uterus in each procedure. The hope is one or more will become viable. If we took this course of action, our doctor might have asked us to 'reduce' the viable babies in order to give better odds to the others. I knew I would never, ever be able to do that. My faith and moral compass would not allow it. All life is precious in God's eyes and it would be up to Him to sort it all out. Not up to me or a doctor.

The second dilemma was this. What if, by some miracle of the Lord, we had early success? What would become of the 'leftover' embryos? My beliefs tell me this is life and a life I would be responsible for. One option presented was those embryos could be destroyed. Clearly that was a no go.

The second option was that we could give them to a couple who could never afford the procedure. While a better option, I still could not reconcile that. Once those embryos were created, I believed myself to be responsible for them. In my mind, giving away those embryo's was no different than carrying a child to term and then giving it away. It's one thing to give a baby up for adoption when it's the right thing for a child. This was entirely different. If we went down this path, we would be intentionally creating life and then walking away from it. I imagined myself forever staring at children that looked like mine and wondering if that child was a sibling to my child. At the end of the day, I just couldn't do it.

The last thing that factored into my decision to not go through with this course of action, was that we already had two children in our lives that were genetically my husband's and not mine. I didn't want to bear a child that also was not genetically mine. The decision was made to pursue adoption. We would raise a child that was not genetically either of ours, or there would be no children.

We didn't pursue adoption right away. We had some things we needed to take care of first. My husband had been medically retired from the Army just a few months after we got married. To help him cope with the medical issue that caused the retirement, doctors had prescribed opioids. A lot of opioids. He became very addicted to them and his personality changed drastically. When we had been married just a little over three years, we came to a crisis point. He was getting sicker and sicker. His body needed more and more of the narcotics. He finally reached a breaking point. We worked with his doctor to wean him off the drugs. It took several weeks, but he was ultimately successful and remains so today.

Six weeks after he got clean, he was diagnosed with testicular cancer. The mystery of what happened to his 'Ranger Sperm' was solved. We fought cancer for two years. He was stage three upon diagnosis. He had 5 surgeries and 6 rounds of chemo. It was a very long and tough battle.

The surgery that actually saved his life had a side effect. We knew going in it could happen, and it did. During the course of the surgery, his Vans Deferens was severed. If you're not familiar with male anatomy, this is a coiled tube that carries sperm out of the testes. I wrote this in my journal the day after we confirmed with his doctor the outcome.

> "The final fertility blow came yesterday. Steve's plumbing was damaged in the surgery so his sperm now goes back into the bladder and not out. Wham! The coffin has been nailed shut on the possibility of me ever being pregnant, God's answer is no. A firm, definite, absolute, complete no.
>
> While I don't understand it, I believe He has my best at heart. It breaks my heart and makes me very sad, but I trust God. Please show me God,

> how to grieve and let go. Show me how to rest in your best."

Early in my infertility journey, I just prayed for a baby. We've already covered the ground of what happened in my first marriage and why it was a blessing no children came of that union. When my second husband and I had so much trouble getting pregnant as well, my prayers changed.

I made these two journal entries two and a half years before we learned God's answer.

> "Please give me your wisdom regarding children. I desire your will more than I desire a child. Am I to be childless? I long for your clear direction."

And:

> "I've been earnestly praying for a yes or a no. Are there to be children, or do I just need to forget about it and move on?"

I really wanted a clear yes or no, and on March 22, 2004 God gave me a very clear answer. That prayer was answered. It wasn't the answer I hoped for. It wasn't what I wanted at all. Eleven years had passed full of disappointment, confusion and heartache. I finally had a definite answer. It was a hard and firm 'no' from the Lord.

Based on the title of this chapter, I imagine you would expect the 'happy ending' to come here. Well, I hate to disappoint you, but that's not what happened. Not all wombs get opened. Mine didn't. But, there are many examples in scripture where the opposite is true. Let's take a look at Hannah.

When God Opens a Womb, Often Someone Prayed

> Then Hannah rose after eating and drinking in Shiloh. Now Eli the priest was sitting on the seat by the doorpost of the temple of the Lord. And she, greatly distressed, prayed to the Lord and wept bitterly. And she made a vow and said, "O LORD of hosts, if thou wilt indeed look on the affliction of Thy maidservant and remember me, and not forget Thy maidservant, but will give Thy maidservant a son, then I will give him to the LORD all the days of his life, and a razor shall never come on his head" (I Sam. 1:9-11).

I love Hannah. I know Hannah's pain. Her husband, Elkanah, loved her deeply. He had two wives: Hannah and Peninnah. Ms. P had all the babies and Hannah had none. 1 Samuel 1:4 says, "And when the day came that Elkanah sacrificed, he would give portions to Peninnah his wife and to *all her sons and daughters*," (italics added). Sounds like Ms. P had enough kids to form a football team and the cheer squad. It wasn't enough for her to just enjoy the blessing she had in all of the children God had given her. Nope. She made Hannah's life miserable by rubbing it in. The King James version says she 'provoked her sore.' Ms. P added to Hannah's sorrow by making fun of her and hurting Hannah with her words. She made Hannah cry.

We know from verse five the Lord closed Hannah's womb. But to Hannah he would give a double portion, for he loved Hannah, but the Lord had closed her womb (1 Sam. 1:5).

As the story continues, Hannah goes to the temple of the Lord. She's distressed, crying bitterly, and praying to God. She pleads with the Lord to give her a son. And then she does something extraordinary. She promises God, if He grants this request, she will give this child back to Him. Hannah was praying silently in her heart, crying out to God with everything in her. It was intense!

Eli, the priest was watching her. She was so engrossed in her pain and pleas that Eli thought she was drunk. That's some serious praying. He confronted Hannah and she explained herself. She didn't tell him what she was praying about, only that she was a woman oppressed in spirit and was pouring out her soul before the Lord.

Eli answered her explanation in verse 1:17 saying this, "….Go in peace; and may the God of Israel grant your petition that you have asked of Him."

Her time with the Lord and the words of the Priest comforted Hannah. Her burden was lifted and she left with hope in her heart. Verse 19 tells us "The Lord remembered her." She conceived and gave birth to a son. She named him Samuel. Once the boy Samuel was old enough to be weaned, she returned with him to the Temple and presented him to the priest, Eli, for service to the Lord. Verse 1:28 says, "So I have also dedicated him to the Lord, as long as he lives he is dedicated to the Lord.' And he worshiped the Lord there."

Wow. This long-awaited, much-loved gift from God was given back to the Lord as promised. That took courage! The pain it must have caused her heart to leave her little boy at the Temple is hard to fathom. This was her first born. And yet, she honored her promise to the Lord, because the Lord answered her prayer with a yes. He saw her pain and He remembered her. He did more than that though. We learn in 1 Samuel 2:21 she had five other children. God rewarded her faithfulness by filling her quiver.

When she delivered Samuel to the Temple, Hannah prayed the following prayer:

> Then Hannah prayed and said,
> "My heart exults in the Lord;
> My horn is exalted in the Lord,
> My mouth speaks boldly against my enemies,
> Because I rejoice in Your salvation.
> There is no one holy like the Lord,
> Indeed, there is no one besides You,
> Nor is there any rock like our God.
> Boast no more so very proudly,
> Do not let arrogance come out of your mouth;
> For the Lord is a God of knowledge,
> And with Him actions are weighed.
> The bows of the mighty are shattered,
> But the feeble gird on strength.
> Those who were full hire themselves out for bread,
> But those who were hungry cease to hunger.
> Even the barren gives birth to seven,
> But she who has many children languishes.
> The Lord kills and makes alive;
> He brings down to Sheol and raises up.
> The Lord makes poor and rich;
> He brings low, He also exalts.
> He raises the poor from the dust,

He lifts the needy from the ash heap
To make them sit with nobles,
And inherit a seat of honor;
For the pillars of the earth are the Lord's,
And He set the world on them.
He keeps the feet of His godly ones,
But the wicked ones are silenced in darkness;
For not by might shall a man prevail.
Those who contend with the Lord will be shattered;
Against them He will thunder in the heavens,
The Lord will judge the ends of the earth;
And He will give strength to His king,
And will exalt the horn of His anointed"
(1 Sam. 2:1-10).

Hannah praised God for who He is. She praised Him for His character. She cites God's strength, His salvation, His holiness, His sovereignty, His fairness and much more. Hannah loved the Giver more than the gift.

The God that answered Hannah's prayer, and gave her a child, is the same God that said no to me. Is he still worthy to be praised in this beautiful manner that Hannah praised Him? Yes!!

When God says 'no', it doesn't mean He doesn't love you. It does not mean He's punishing you for something. What it means is that His ways are not our ways. He sees the long game. We only see the present. He sees the past, the present and the future. He always has your best at heart. God is a God who sees. He knows the heartache and the deep pain of the childless woman. And it matters to Him. A lot. He has a reason for it. Trust that. I promise you there is a reason. You may never know what it is this side of heaven. But still, trust that God does not close a womb without a really good reason and it is a really, really, big deal for Him to do so.

We see many examples in scripture where God heard the prayer of someone asking for children. Remember what happened with the household of Abimelech? Because of Sarah and Abraham's bad choices God closed up all of the wombs.

And Abraham prayed to God; and God healed Abimelech and his wife and his maids, so that they bore children. For the Lord had closed fast all the wombs of the household of Abimelech because of Sarah, Abraham's wife (Gen. 20:17-18).

We'll talk more about this in chapter 7, but God and Abraham had several conversations about Sarah's closed womb. God heard Abraham's prayers and opened Sarah's womb.

Abraham's daughter-in-law, Rebekah was barren. In Genesis 25:21 we read, "And Isaac prayed to the Lord on behalf of his wife, because she was barren; and the Lord answered him and Rebekah his wife conceived."

We know Zacharias prayed for his wife Elizabeth to have a child. Luke 1:13 says, "But the angel said to him, 'Do not be afraid, Zacharias, for your petition has been heard, and your wife Elizabeth will bear you a son, and you will give him the name John.'"

When God opens a womb, often someone prayed.

Chapter 5
Nothing is Impossible with God

My Closure

As you can imagine, we were exhausted. We were physically drained and emotionally wiped out. Let's re-cap just a bit. We had been married five years at the conclusion of the Ranger's cancer treatment. In those five years, he lost his military career due to health problems, battled opioid addiction, we started a business together, we went through infertility treatment and spent two years battling cancer. We needed to get off the emotional roller coaster and take a break.

In January, a few months after his last treatment, he indicated he wasn't sure if he was still interested in adopting. I told him we were going to take a break for the year. We needed to get healed up; physically and emotionally. We would revisit the idea at that time. I was 41. That December, we spent Christmas with his family in Florida. We decided to go to Disney World while on the trip. His mom, his daughter, his sister and her kids all went with us.

The first day, just as we walked through the doors of the Magic Kingdom, my phone rang. It was the wife of the pastor who married us. We're friends, but they were living in a different state. It was unusual to get a call from her. I answered. After a brief exchange of the usual niceties, she told me about a young girl in their church who was pregnant and was considering putting the baby up for adoption. My friend and her husband both felt led to reach out to us and see if we wanted to be considered as possible adoptive parents. "Were we interested?" she asked.

That kind of call will stop you dead in your tracks. I told her I would get back to her. I filled my husband in on the purpose of the call. We spent the next two days staring at children of all ages. We noticed the sleeping, peaceful ones. We noticed the screaming, 'I'm done with Disney today' ones. We stared with near terror at the children who seemed to have an unlimited amount of energy and their tired, exhausted parents. And we asked ourselves the question, "Were we interested?"

YES! We didn't pursue this. It came to us a year after we said we'd table the conversation. We believed it to be from the Lord. Not pursuing it felt like it could be a rejection of God's perfect gift in God's perfect time. We learned what we needed to do, which agency she was using, put our packet together and sent it off to the agency. That was in January.

Several months went by and we didn't hear anything. In the meantime, we had the opportunity to count the cost of how much our lives would change. There's a reason young people have children. When you're older and wiser you understand reality. This was going to be hard. Glorius and magical and hard.

While we waited, my nephews wife and 18-month-old daughter stayed with us for about 4 weeks. (My nephew was deployed to Afghanistan). Having a wee one in the house was at the same time a wonderful blessing and a real eye opener. She got sick for a couple of days during her stay and her mom told me she had pretty bad diarrhea. I changed many a diaper in my day with nieces and nephews, but the concept of baby diarrhea had never even occurred to me.

We played with baby Amy, took her trick or treating, laughed at her antics and were grateful when she woke up screaming at night that her mom was the one who had to deal with it. Even so, the day they left to go back home, I cried and cried. That little girl is all grown up now and she has a special bond with me and the Ranger.

During the three-month period of waiting, I realized something very important. I was totally neutral on adopting this baby. Given the opportunity to take that child into my home and raise it, I totally would, and love it as if it was my own. I also realized, if it didn't work out, I was fine. I no longer felt I needed to have or raise a baby to feel complete.

When the call came that the girl and her parents had decided to keep the baby, my husband was surprised at my lack of disappointment. Well, first of all, I had nearly 15 years of protecting my heart from the hope of a child. More importantly though, I realized God brought us into this situation to give me closure. That's what a caring and loving God does. I was a month away from 42 and let's be real, I could barely get myself out of bed in the morning, let alone me and a newborn.

I made this journal entry on March 2, 2006, two years after learning I would never become pregnant:

> "As I write this morning, the sounds of my great-niece Amy drift up through the vent. Her squeals of joy are a wonderful soothing balm to my heart and soul. Amy and her mom have been staying with us for a few weeks. There was a problem in their home that rendered it unlivable for a time. They should be back home in a week or so, once the repairs have been made. It has been a delight having them here.
>
> We found out this week that Abby is keeping her baby. We are disappointed, but not devastated. I'm assuming this is the final chapter in our quest for a child. Neither of us feel led to pursue a different adoption. This one pursued us, which is what made it special. One of the things that came from this experience was the unity Steve and I experienced through the entire decision-making process. Another thing for me was the opportunity to examine in a very realistic, mature, grown-up way what it would really mean to introduce a baby into our lives. As a dear friend said, "Count the cost." Having sweet Amy here has really helped me do that as well. (God's timing is perfect).

While the reality of parenting doesn't repel me, it doesn't draw me in anymore either. I'm neutral on wanting to parent now, at nearly 42 years of age. And at the same time, I grieve the loss of never having borne a child into this world to love and raise and send off. I guess the phrase 'mixed emotions' really summarizes how I feel. I'm okay to not parent now, but sad I never really got to have that blessing and challenge. I am grateful to God for giving me the circumstances to examine more deeply than I ever have, the reality of parenting. And, I'm grateful for the friends and family who prayed with us through this short-lived experience."

Nothing is Impossible with God

> In the days of Herod, king of Judea, there was a priest named Zacharias, of the division of Abijah; and he had a wife from the daughters of Aaron, and her name was Elizabeth. They were both righteous in the sight of God, walking blamelessly in all the commandments and requirements of the Lord. But they had no child, because Elizabeth was barren, and they were both advanced in years (Luke 1:5-7).

Elizabeth and Zacharias had good stats. They were both descendants of Aaron, Moses' brother. These scriptures tell us they were also both blameless before the Lord, were careful to carry out his commandments and live right. Elizabeth was barren, so the fact they were old was a problem. Things didn't look good for them on the baby-making front. God closes wombs for many reasons, some knowable and some not, but it's important to point out Elizabeth was not barren due to anybody's sin. It was simply that God had some big plans in mind!

Zacharias was away from home working at the Temple. We know from Luke 1:39 he and Elizabeth lived in the 'hill country, in a city of Judah'. The Temple was in Jerusalem. He was doing his job and it seemed to just be an ordinary day at work. Then the extraordinary happened!

Through the luck of the draw, Zacharias was chosen that day to enter the Temple of the Lord and burn incense. Incense symbolizes the prayers of the nation of Israel, so it's not a big leap to think he was praying while the incense burned. We know from Luke 1:10 a bunch of people were outside praying 'during the hour of incense offering', so it's likely he was too. Since he was away from home, he may have been missing Elizabeth. One source I read went so far as to suggest maybe in that moment he was praying for a son or for the coming of the Messiah.[8]

In the middle of the incense offering, Gabriel, the angel of the Lord, appeared next to the alter of incense. Gabe often shows up when God has a big announcement. This time is no exception. Gabe tells Zacharias several things. First of all, he says 'don't be afraid'. Luke 1:12 tells us Zacharias was gripped with fear, so Gabe needed him to settle down a bit in order to receive the message. Next, Gabe says Zacharias' prayers have been heard! It had to be comforting and humbling all at once to know the God who created the universe heard his prayers. Gabe says Elizabeth is going to have a baby and he will be named John.

That in and of itself would be a lot to take in. But it just gets better. Gabe goes on to tell Zacharias how special Baby John is going to be. He will drink no wine or liquor. He will be great in the sight of the Lord. He will be filled with the Holy Spirit while in his mother's womb. He will turn back many sons of Israel to the Lord. And, this is the big one, He will be a forerunner to the Messiah in the spirit and power of Elijah, and will turn the hearts of the fathers back to the children. Wait. What?! The Messiah is eminent!!

Let's unpack all of these statements about John. The fact that no wine or liquor will ever touch his lips is an indication of a Nazarite vow. Some would take this vow for a period of time and it indicates one is set apart for a special service to God during that time. A Nazarite dressed differently, ate a different

---

8 Pg. 204, Bible Knowledge Commentary

diet (locusts and honey), didn't cut his hair and generally stayed away from the normal creature comforts of society. The message seemed to be that John would live his entire life this way, not just for a period of time.

There are three instances in scripture where the parents dedicate the child for a life time of service to God in this manner; John the Baptist, Hannah's Samuel and the parents of Samson. Scripture tells us Samson was born to begin to deliver Israel from the hand of the Philistines. Samuel was a prophet, priest and judge. John the Baptist came to prepare the way for the ministry of Jesus, the Messiah. Oh, and fun fact, all three of these mothers were barren until God opened their womb for the purpose of furthering His Kingdom.

When Gabe tells Zacharias John will 'function in the spirit of Elijah and will turn hearts', he's quoting two different prophecies in Malachi. (Malachi 3:1 and 4:5-6) Those scriptures tell of the return of Elijah before the Messiah comes and that there will be a front runner before the Messiah, to prepare the way for Him. Zacharias knew those scriptures. This celestial being is telling him he's going to have a son who fulfills both of those prophecies.

Shut the front door!! This is a big deal. A big message. A huge proclamation, delivered to a really good and righteous man who loves God. His response?

Prove it.

I'm old. My wife's old. Prove it to me.

Can you blame him really? God had been silent for 400 years. No one knew that better than Zacharias the priest. He'd likely been praying for years for a son. That in and of itself would have been enough for him and Elizabeth. But to be told you're going to have a son and he's going to be a fulfillment of prophesy that comes before another fulfillment of prophecy? It's just a lot.

The Angel Gabriel answered him with authority! Luke 1:18 says in part, "...I am Gabriel, who stands in the presence of God; and I have been sent to speak to you, and to bring you this good news." It kind of reads like, "Do you *know* who I am?!" Zacharias gets put in a time out of sorts until the baby is born. Because he doubted the message from Gabriel, he is unable to speak until John is born and circumcised.

Meanwhile, the large group of people outside praying during the hour of the incense sacrifice were wondering what was taking so long. They were waiting on him to reappear and when he did, they realized he'd seen a vision based on the fact he couldn't speak and was explaining himself with hand gestures. Luke 1:23 tells us he finished up his priestly duties and then went back home. Sure enough, Elizabeth gets pregnant. Scripture tells us she kept in seclusion for five months. No one but the happy couple knew she was pregnant. She would have gotten a lot of attention at the miracle of it all. Maybe she just wanted to avoid that and savor the journey in private for as long as she could.

There's another part of this story that just begs to be included, even though it's not about a barren woman. It's in fact, about a virgin woman. When Elizabeth was 6 months pregnant, the Angel Gabriel was once again deployed by God to a city in Galilee, called Nazareth. There he visited a young woman who was engaged to a young man, Joseph. Her name was Mary. And this is what Gabriel said.

"....Hail favored one! The Lord is with you." "...Do not be afraid, Mary; for you have found favor with God. And behold, you will conceive in your womb, and bear a son, and you shall name him Jesus. He will be great and will be called the Son of the Most High; and the Lord God will give Him the throne of His father David; and He will reign over the house of Jacob forever, and His Kingdom shall have no end" (Luke 1:28, 30-33).

Mary's response was a little different than Zacharias. She was filled with wonderment and awe. Her only question was how. How is this going to work, since I'm a virgin? She believed the message. She just was curious as to the mechanics of the deal. We see this in the first chapter of Luke.

And the angel answered and said to her, "The Holy Spirit will come upon you , and the power of the Most High will overshadow you; and for that reason the holy offspring shall be called the Son of God. And behold, even your relative Elizabeth has also conceived a son in her old age; and she who was called barren is now in her sixth month. *For nothing will be impossible with God,*" (Luke 1:35-37 italics and underline added).

We don't know the age of Elizabeth and Zacharias, but we do know the age of Sarah and Abraham. Scripture tells us in Genesis, Abraham was 100 and Sarah was 90. This is why they both laughed. Abraham 'fell on his face and laughed in Chapter 17. Sarah was a little more polite about it 'laughing to herself' in Chapter 18, but they both laughed at the earthly impossibility of it all. And then God said in Genesis 18:19a, *"Is anything too difficult for the Lord?"* (italics and underline added).

God can do the impossible. He can open the wombs of old women. He can bring about a virgin birth. He is God, after all.

We also see in this story that Zacharias prayed. God heard His prayer and answered it with a yes. And the timing of it was all God. God picked a specific moment in history when the Messiah would come. He chose Mary of Nazareth to be the virgin mother of Jesus. God chose a couple whose child would be destined to become a priest because of his lineage, to be a new kind of priest, to spread the good news of Jesus before his ministry began. Opening or closing Elizabeth's womb any earlier or later would have thrown off the timeline. God's timing is always perfect. Nothing is too difficult for God. Nothing is impossible with God.

Chapter 6
The Empty Womb is a Big Deal to God

My Empty Arms

I'm sure dear reader, you're still rooting for a miracle, since nothing is impossible with God. I hate to disappoint you, but no. I was never able to have children and we didn't adopt. I'm a woman with empty arms. I found this in my journal, 11 years after I first started trying to get pregnant.

> *"I need thee, oh I need thee, every hour I need thee."*

My journal entry continued:

> "I dream sometimes of what it would be like to tell my mother I'm going to give her a grand-

child. What joy that would bring her (and me)! It would be so fun. I daydream about being pregnant, going through childbirth, holding my newborn in my arms, nursing for the first time, spending entire days playing with and caring for my child…going to the zoo, reading to my child, going for walks in the stroller, teaching them to ride a bike, a horse and to drive. I imagine a fun, easy going relationship-where my child grows up loved, accepted, confident, successful, humble… so many dreams left unrealized. God has a plan He will unveil in His time.

'In His time, In His time, God makes everything wonderful in His time.'"

And on the same day, this….

"My Arms are Empty
No child rests there
No child in my care
No child suckles the breast
No child breathes sweet breath
My arms are empty

No child sleeps in the crib
No child gurgles in a bib
No child coos in the night
No child greets me with delight
My arms are empty

No child calls me Mom
No child to keep from harm
No child plays with glee
No child of mine do I see
My arms are empty

No child to raise right
No child growing up bright
No child rests there
No child in my care
My arms are empty

But, my heart is full of joy and
    hope in the Lord
My heart waits expectantly
for the Lord's hand to move upon me.
As Hannah, Elizabeth, Sarah, and Rebekkah
I wait for my Samuel, my John, my Isaac,
    or Jacob
Each one a gift from the Lord
Greatly anticipated and greatly adored.
A mighty plan for each had He
His timing perfectly
laid down before time began.
God's timing, of course, must be ran.

The waiting is hard.
The trusting harder still.
But above all I desire the Lord's perfect will.
For He is El Roi, he sees my plight.

My heart is full of joy and in the Lord I delight
My heart waits expectantly
To conceive in the night
A child to fill my arms
Created by God's might."

It would be another four years after penning this I learned I would never become pregnant and two years after that, God would bring closure to me in my quest to become a mother, when I chose not to pursue adoption. Even with closure and peace, I'm still mindful of a sense of loss and all of the things I will never experience; that look of a babe in arms gazing into her mother's eyes, the joy of the firsts and milestones – steps, teeth, days of school, dates, graduations and weddings, time with grandchildren, time with adult children in middle age and old age. I just don't get to do these things or have these experiences.

In her book, *'Spoken from the Heart'* Laura Bush, who had a great deal of trouble conceiving, writes these words. "The English language lacks the words to mourn an absence. For the loss of a parent, grandparent, spouse, child or friend, we have all manner of words and phrases, some helpful, some not. Still, we are conditioned to say something, even if it is only 'I am sorry for your loss.' But for an absence, for someone who was never there at all, we are wordless to capture that particular emptiness. For those who deeply want children and are denied them, the missing babies hover like silent, ephemeral shadows over their lives. Who can describe the feel of a tiny hand that is never held?" [9]

Such a powerful description of the struggle. How do you grieve the loss of something, or in this case, someone, you never had? I truly do have peace and closure, but that does not mean there is no pain, no sense of loss.

Mother's Day is still hard. In the days leading up to that day, and even on that day, so many well-meaning people wish women a Happy Mother's Day. They don't know. They are being kind. It's a little stab in my heart each and every time, I choose to graciously smile and say thank you, rather than tell them I'm not a mother. The one 'Happy Mother's Day' greeting that makes my day each year is the one that comes from my step-daughter. She has a wonderful adoring mother, but that act of respect each year, is heart warming to me. The others are just hard.

Next to Psalm 127 in my Message Bible, I have this note, written on November 17, 2017, twenty-four years after I began my quest to become a mother and eleven years after the quest ended, "This always makes me a little sad – empty quiver/empty womb."

Proverbs 30:15b and 16a says this, "There are three things that will not be satisfied, four that will not say, 'Enough': Sheol and the barren womb..." Peace and closure may come, but the longing does not end. Ever.

---

9 Pg. 104, Spoken from the Heart, Laura Bush

I'm not the first woman to struggle with this issue and I won't be the last. As hard as it is, I have determined there truly are worse things in the world that could happen to someone than not having a child. The list is long in this fallen world we live in, of 'worse things'. I have my own list of 'worse things'. I'll leave it to you to choose your list of 'worse things'.

Life is a series of losses and griefs. One grieves the loss of a dream. And God gives a new dream. One grieves the loss of hope. Hopelessness is a very deep grief and raw emotion. It physically hurts. Proverbs 13:12a says "Hope deferred makes the heart sick…" But God tells us our hope is to be in Him. Psalms 31:24 says, "Be strong, and let your heart take courage, all you who hope in the Lord."

Behold, the eye of the Lord is on those who fear Him, On those who hope for His lovingkindness. Let Thy lovingkindness, O Lord, be upon us, According as we have hoped in Thee (Psalms 33:18,22).

Why are you in despair, O my soul? And why have you become disturbed within me? Hope in God, for I shall again praise Him For the help of His presence (Psalm 42:5).

Why are you in despair, O my soul? And why are you disturbed within me? Hope in God, for I shall again praise Him, the help of my countenance and my God (Psalm 43:5)

Next to this last verse I have written this note, "Why does your heart despair, when you should be praising God!"

I'm not at all suggesting there should be no grieving. It's important to grieve the loss of something (motherhood) or someone (a child who never came). Scripture is full of grief, Psalms especially. Hannah grieved. Rachel grieved. Grieving, with a focus on God for who He is will protect your heart from becoming bitter. Bitterness will destroy you from the inside out. If you've become bitter, give that over to God and let him relieve you of it. Ask God to replace the bitterness with contentment in your circumstance and delight in Him.

In my grieving, I've chosen to focus on the goodness of God. I trust in who He is, not what He does or doesn't do for me. God is kind, gracious, and wise. He knows me intimately –just like the woman with the blood issue, even the hairs on my head are numbered. (Matthew 10:30). It was He who knit me together in my own mother's womb, tilted uterus and all. (Psalm 139:13). He knew when He made me this would be my struggle and how it would end.

I'd like to know why, but I don't have to know why to know God is good. Romans 8:28 tells us "And we know that God causes all things to work together for good to those who love God, to those who are called according to His purpose." All things! Not some things. All things. Even not ever having children. All things. I trust God has a reason for closing my womb. Sometimes I wonder if it's a little bit like the line from the movie *A Few Good Men*, where Jack Nicholson's character barks, "You want the truth? You can't handle the truth!" Maybe, just maybe, my lack of knowing why is to protect me from what I don't need to know and can't handle right now. God is just that good.

In His goodness and love, He brought us into a 'near adoption' situation just to give me closure. In His goodness and love He began to show me these truths in scripture I write about here, over twenty years before I would pen them for you. In His goodness and love, He has walked with me every step of the way, comforted me and held me at the worst of times. And now, because He is a God who never wastes experiences, He has me writing and speaking on this topic to help and encourage other women. That is a God who sees and a God who takes the opening and closing of wombs very seriously.

The Closed Womb is a Really Big Deal to God

> Then the Lord took note of Sarah as He had said, and the Lord did for Sarah as He had promised. So Sarah conceived and bore a son to Abraham in his old age, the appointed time of which God had spoken to him. And Abraham called the name of his son, who was born to him, whom Sarah bore to him, Isaac. Then Abraham circumcised his son Isaac when he was eight days old, as God had commanded him. Now Abraham was one hundred years old when his son Isaac was born to him. And Sarah said, "God has made laughter for me; everyone who hears will laugh with me." And she said, "Who would have said to Abraham that Sarah would nurse children? Yet I have borne him a son in his old age" (Gen. 21:1-7).

When we last left Sarah and Abraham, they were in trouble with Abimelech for running a con about who Sarah was to Abraham. Abraham was praying to God to open up the wombs in Abimelech's household. We saw in previous chapters God's promises to Abraham; that his descendants would be too numerous to count, his descendants would inhabit Canaan and these descendants would come through Isaac, the child Sarah would have in her old age.

In Chapter 21, God comes through with the promise of a child from 90 year old Sarah. The story of Sarah and Abraham demonstrate all five of the principles I write about in this book. Let's take the last one first: the empty womb is a big deal to God.

The first thing we learn about Sarah, besides she married Abraham, was that she was barren. It's actually two phrases, one sentence, in one verse.

And Sarah was barren; she had no child (Gen. 11:30).

There's a great deal of emphasis put on this fact.

We see a similar emphasis put on Elizabeth's barrenness in Luke. After scripture tells us about their good character in the eyes of the Lord, we see another verse devoted to Elizabeth's state of barrenness.

And they had no child, because Elizabeth was barren, and they were advanced in years (Luke 1:7).

When we learn this fact about Sarah, she was young, a virtual newlywed. They were just getting started in life, but the Bible tells us right away, she was barren. This is an important fact in the story.

Elizabeth though, she's already long in the tooth when scripture tells us she's barren, as noted in verse 7. Luke pays special attention to this fact, because again, it's important to the story.

In 1 Samuel, there are not one, but two verses dedicated to telling us about Hannah's barrenness. We learn Hannah was loved, but barren in verse 1:5 and Hannah was picked on by her husband's other wife because the Lord had closed her womb, in 1:6.

Genesis 25 brings us around to the story of Isaac and Rebekkah. It's a long story as to how Isaac found Rebekkah as a wife, and not relevant to this book. What is relevant is verse 25:20 tells us Isaac was 40 when he took Rebekkah as his wife. Then verse 21 tells us this.

And Isaac prayed to the Lord on behalf of his wife, because she was barren; and the Lord answered him and Rebekah his wife conceived. (Gen. 25:21).

In this one we get the picture of barrenness and the answer to prayer all in one fell swoop! Yet again, though, a whole verse set aside to tell us the state of Rebekah's womb.

Genesis 29 gives us information on Rachel and Leah, Jacob's wives.

Now the Lord saw that Leah was unloved, and He opened her womb, but Rachel was barren. (Gen. 29:31).

Just like Hannah and Miss P in 1 Samuel, one was loved and one was not. The unloved had an open, fertile womb, the loved wife had a closed womb.

In regard to Abimelech's household, Genesis 20:18 says, "For the Lord had closed fast all the wombs of the household of Abimelech because of Sarah, Abraham's wife."

And lastly, is a scripture we haven't looked at yet, Judges 13.

And there was a certain man of Zorah, of the family of the Danites, whose name was Manoah; and his wife was barren and had borne no children (Judges 13:2).

Here's a man, from the tribe of Dan, whose wife was barren. Scripture not only tells us this about her in verse 2, but in verse 3 says this:

> Then the angel of the Lord appeared to the woman, and said to her, 'Behold now, you are barren and have borne no children, but you shall conceive and give birth to a son' (Judges 13:3).

These are Samson's parents, one of the three dedicated to the service of the Lord from birth.

What I want the reader to see here is what a big deal it is to God. The wombs of these women were closed up tighter than a drum and God makes note of it in scripture over and over again. God doesn't just run around willy, nilly closing up wombs for the heck of it. When He makes that choice, it is a really big deal to Him and scripture bears that out. The closed womb is a really big deal to God.

I mentioned at the beginning of this chapter, the story of Sarah and Abraham contains all five of the principles I write about in this book. Sarah's closed womb had a purpose. That purpose is to prove one of the other principles; nothing is impossible with God. The impossible became possible when a 100 year old man, got his 90 year old wife pregnant. We also see these two truths bear out in Elizabeth and Zacharias story. Because Luke makes a point to include the fact they are advanced in age, it is made even more miraculous. Both of these examples show us there is no earthly way these two couples could have become pregnant. Both pregnancies came about in such a way it was obvious it was God doing it.

There was another reason too. The opening of Sarah's womb had a purpose. Same for Elizabeth! The opening of their wombs, when they were opened, was God keeping His word and bringing about a promise. He told Sarah and Abraham she would have a baby in a year. God kept His promise and opened her womb just as He said He would, and *when* He said He would. God was also keeping a promise to Abraham that his many descendants would come through the son he would have with Sarah.

Elizabeth's pregnancy with John the Baptist was a different promise being kept. It was one made way back to Abraham! We see this promise in Genesis 12:3b, "And in you all the families of the earth shall be blessed." This is the promise of the Messiah, to come through Abraham's descendant's, bringing salvation to all of the world! While Elizabeth would not carry the Messiah, she would carry and birth the promised forerunner to the Messiah's arrival. God chose the timing of it all. Make no mistake, the open womb of Elizabeth had a big purpose!

In like manner, as we've already seen, the open womb of Rachel and Leah, brought forth the twelve tribes of Israel. The open womb of Hannah and Manoah's wife brought forth male children, Samuel and Samson, with a special purpose in service to Israel.

The last principle that Sarah and Abraham's story shows us is when a womb is open, often someone prayed. God and Abraham talked about Abraham's descendants four times between Genesis 11 and 20. The rubber really meets the road in Genesis 17 when God specifically tells Abraham his many descendants will come through Isaac, the child Sarah is yet to have. They didn't just talk it over. God gave Abraham details.

We know Zacharias prayed, because the angel Gabriel told him his petition had been heard. Genesis 25:21 tells us Isaac prayed for Rebekkah to have children because she was barren. She not only got pregnant, she had twins. She got a double portion!

Hannah poured her heart out before the Lord. She didn't just pray, she pleaded and bargained. God answered her prayer by giving her Samuel. And then she had other children as well!

Genesis 30:24 tells us Rachel named her first born Joseph and then asked the Lord for another son. Her prayers were answered many years later, but sadly, she died bringing little Benjamin into this world.

Not every fervent, heart-felt prayer for a womb to be open is answered with a 'yes.' Sometimes the answer is no. Not every womb gets opened. That in no way means there is a reason to be ashamed. That in no way means God loves you less than the woman with children. That in no way means you're being punished for something. God just doesn't operate that way. Thoughts like that are lies from the deceiver who wants to put a wedge between you and the Lord. This is the same Lord who wants nothing more than to have a personal, intimate relationship with you.

It's often said in Christian circles there are three answers to prayer; yes, no and wait. It's human nature to not like 'wait' and 'no'. Waiting is hard. No is even harder. God is a kind and loving God. Focusing on His character and His truths found in the love letter He wrote us called the Bible, removes the focus from what one doesn't have to the good and loving Father He is. It's called contentment. Not joy. Not happiness. Contentment. Settling into the pocket of life with God at the helm.

It can take some time to get to a place of contentment, whatever the issue you are facing. Digging into scripture and uncovering what God had to say about infertility and barrenness made all the difference for me. I pray it makes a difference for you. Know this, my friend. The closed womb is a really big deal to God.

Chapter 7
Every Journey is Unique

My Saga Continued

This chapter wasn't supposed to be in this book. I intended it to end at chapter 6. Then something strange happened as I was writing the story God gave me to write. I had a new development. Let me lay the groundwork first.

A year or two after the quest to adopt ended, I began once again to have problems with my cycles. I was having very heavy bleeding, and two weeklong cycles. My primary care doctor sent me to a specialist who put me on a very strong birth control pill. I found this funny, since I hadn't used any type of birth control for nearly 20 years. But hey, it did the trick. For 10 years, I had normal and very light cycles.

The year I was 52, my primary care doctor told me in my annual checkup I needed to come off the pill. This was in the fall. The conversation went like this.

"Audrey, you need to come off the birth control pill," she announced.

"Why?" I asked.

"To see if you're in menopause," she answered.

"I'm not having any symptoms," I explained.

"That's because you're on the pill," she retorted.

"And your point is....," I chuckled a bit.

"It's not good for you," she explained.

"Okay, I'll make you a deal. I have five months left on this prescription. When it runs out, I won't ask for it to be renewed. Fair?" I bargained.

She didn't like it but agreed to my 'terms'. I took my last birth control pill on February 14th the following year. I would turn 53 in April. Within two weeks there was no doubt I was in full blown menopause. Hot flashes, night sweats and insomnia began immediately. I've never had a menstrual cycle since. With the history I had up to that point, it's a miracle I got through menopause naturally, with all of those defective parts still in place.

I tried to suck it up for about six weeks, but cried uncle and requested hormone replacement to bring the hot flashes and night sweats under control. I have taken that medication for six years. I thought my problems were over. No more dysfunctional bleeding. No more infertility issues. No more anything!

And then on New Year's Day, of the year I was to finish this book, I started spotting. It was as if my body was saying, "Happy New Year! I fooled you!"

Okay, that's weird, I thought to myself. I had my annual check up ten days later and mentioned it to my doctor. A pelvic ultrasound was ordered. Four fibroid cysts inside my uterus were found, along with a 'somewhat abnormally thick lining', a calcified left ovary and a 'normal' right ovary. I was referred to Gynecology. This doctor called and requested I get in as soon as possible for a uterine biopsy. Yes, it's as awful as it sounds. The doctor did not suspect cancer and the results have come back confirming that to be the case. That's the good news I suppose.

He wants to take me off the hormone replacement and leave all of those defective, useless organs inside of me. This will likely stop the spotting and cause the fibroids to dissipate. I want something all together different. I want them gone. The ovaries. The tubes. The uterus. All of it. I want it out. We'll see who wins this debate. I suspect it may be me. I made a pretty good case for a hysterectomy in the biopsy appointment.

Here's the thing that really surprised me. I suppose, because I have spent the last several weeks really focused on writing this book, telling my story and all of the many difficult emotional and physical things I've endured, I have very raw emotion about this latest turn of events. Rational or not, I'm MAD at my ovaries, tubes and uterus! They have been the bane of my existence since I was in my mid 20's. I'm 59 at the publishing of this book.

I'm angry at what they've put me through. As punishment, I believe they should be banished! Knowing what I know about my body, I truly believe if not removed, I will be right back here in a few months or years, having the same conversation with a different doctor. I will be older and recovery from the hysterectomy that so needs to happen, will be made even more difficult. The verse in Mark, regarding the woman with the blood issue keeps coming to mind. "She had endured much at the hands of doctors."

During the uterine biopsy, which is as painful as it is humiliating, I got through it by taking slow and deliberate breaths, dabbing a tissue to my eyes as I wept quietly…just a little, and calling out to El Roi, the God who sees me. I silently prayed for Him to give me the strength to endure the procedure. I knew going in what I was facing. I had this done years ago in my infertility journey. I don't know which doctor. I don't remember at what stage it was done. Safe to say, it was not something I ever wanted to remember and certainly didn't expect to ever have to endure again. The doctor even asked me when the procedure was completed if I'd had this test before, as it was something they used to perform for infertility treatment. I told him yes and went on to say, if there is a procedure known to mankind for infertility, I guarantee I've had it done.

When he left the room, the sweet nurse stayed behind to clean up the room. I lost it a little. Through my tears, I explained I was likely more emotional than I normally would have been because of this book. I told her what the book was about and that I was writing it to encourage women who had a similar struggle. I wanted to let them know what God had to say on the matter. Turns out she is a believer! How wonderful of God to put a sweet, Christian woman in the room with me right when

I needed it most! Oh, and she wore cowboy boots and western jeans. My kind of gal!

No one is more surprised than me to find my journey surrounding the barren womb continuing at this age. It got me thinking though, about each of the women I've discussed in the pages of this book what their journeys looked like. Let's take a look at those unique journeys, the fertile and the barren, to close out this book.

Each Journey is Unique

Sarah had the longest journey. She likely married when she was a teenager. This would have made her wait to have a baby 70-75 years! That's a lifetime. Little wonder she got impatient and took matters into her own hands, asking her husband to sleep with her maid Hagar. Genesis 16 tells us a lot of things about this choice. When she was in her mid-70's, Sarah gave Hagar to her husband as a wife.

Even though it was her idea, she was very angry with Hagar and treated her harshly, just for doing what Sarah asked of her. Maybe Sarah was Jealous. Maybe she was mad at herself for coming up with this idea. Maybe she was mad at Abraham. This guy put Sarah in compromising positions at least twice we know of. The fact that she went along with it, doesn't negate how hurtful it may have been to her. When it came to Hagar, she may have really wanted Abraham to just say no and to honor her for once in his life. Whatever she was feeling, she took it out on poor Hagar.

It got so bad, Hagar took off on her own. A very risky thing to do in the wilderness. The angel of the Lord, (there He is again!) came to her as she sat near a spring and chatted with her. He told Hagar to go back home. He promised her she would have many descendants and told her that her son will be a 'wild donkey of a man'. This guy is going to be trouble. He's going to fight everyone and will live 'east' of his brothers. Abraham and Ishmael are considered the fathers of the Muslim faith. Talk about choices having consequences. The entire planet is still fighting the fight started between two women over infertility.

Oh, and Hagar did go back. She even hung out a few years. After Isaac was born, Sarah saw Ishmael mocking. Scripture doesn't say who or what exactly, but I'm guessing it was Isaac. That was that. Sarah insisted Abraham send Hagar and Ishmael away. And he did. Seems like Ishmael had cause to be angry at the world. His dad disowned him and his mother. Sent her off with some water and bread (Genesis chapters 16 and 21). Not cool Abraham. But let's get back to Sarah.

Sarah lost hope. She gave up. She lost faith in her God. And she did what most of us do when that happens. She decided she knew better than God and she took action. I wonder how different the world would be if she had just waited on the Lord?

Ultimately, she had the miracle baby Isaac and even lived long enough to get him raised. Scripture tells us Sarah lived to 127 years of age. Isaac would have been 37 years old when his mother died. God didn't just give her a baby. She got to raise him too! While there is a happy ending for Sarah, her journey was one of impatience, jealousy, anger and vengeance. Even so, God blessed her and Abraham. Just goes to show, if we love Him and follow Him, God *doesn't* give us what we deserve.

Rachel followed a similar path. Jacob loved his wife Rachel. He had to fight to get her. What woman wouldn't love that?! But, she was the second wife, not the first as she was supposed to be. And she didn't bear him sons. Rachel became jealous. She started the blame game. It was Jacob's fault! She was having quite the pity party. They had an ugly fight. She too took matters into her own hands and offered up her maid as a wife for Jacob.

Cultural norm or not, where's the man who says NO! I love you and I don't want to lay with another woman? He did what his grandfather did and took a third wife. To make matters worse, she offered Bilhah in anger and Jacob acted in anger. This can't have helped their already strained marriage any. Bilhah had two sons for Rachel and Jacob, so clearly it wasn't a one and done.

At long last, God gave Rachel a son. Sweet Joseph. One of the heroes of the Bible. But Rachel never knew that. She didn't get the pleasure of knowing what a fine young man he grew to be. She didn't live to know how he saved the whole family and God's chosen people. Rachel wanted another son so badly. Sometimes God gives us what we ask for, even when it may not be the best thing for us. She got pregnant again, but as we learned before, died in childbirth bringing Joseph's brother Benjamin into the world. God could have used any one of the other women in Jacob's life to bring the twelfth son for the twelve tribes. But He chose Rachel. She lost her life getting what she wanted. The bigger tragedy here is she was buried along the side of the road as they travelled. She didn't make it into the family tomb. Rachel didn't act with honor and at the end of the day, she wasn't treated with honor by her husband.

Rebekkah, Isaac's wife starts out so sweet! Abraham sends one of his servants to his homeland to find a wife for Isaac. He is successful right away. The story is told in Genesis 24. The servant finds her and gets her father to agree to take her back to Canaan to marry Isaac. She must have been brave and adventurous to take on the unknown like this. It didn't take much convincing before Rebekkah and her nurse Deborah were headed back to Canaan. It seems it was love at first sight upon their arrival. Isaac loved Rebekkah and took her as his wife.

Scripture doesn't tell us much about her infertility journey. There's only one verse that says she's barren, Isaac prayed, God answered his prayer and Rebekkah got pregnant with twins. This is where we begin to see a different side of Rebekkah. The twins couldn't be more different. Esau was ruddy, hairy and outdoorsy. He was a hunter. Isaac related more to him than Jacob. Jacob was Rebekkah's favorite. Jacob was a conniver and deceiver. He may have learned that from his mom. She was the one who coached him through how to steal Esau's blessing. She was the one who found out Esau wanted to kill him for this and helped him get away. She was the one who insisted he take a wife from her people and sent Jacob there. He left on the run and running for his life. Partly because of what he'd done and partly because of what his mom helped him do.

She may have had a sweet and loving side. But she also had a spirit of adventure and defiance. Rebekkah was not afraid to rock the boat and do things that would help her favorite son at the expense of the other.

❧

Peninnah is a mean, bitter woman. Her womb was open and she was having all of the babies. But she was unloved by her husband. She picked on her rival, Hannah something awful. She made Hannah cry. Hannah tells us in 1 Samuel 2:5 that 'she who has many children languishes.' Miss P is miserable in her own skin. What a sad and lonely journey. She could have had a great friend in Hannah, but instead made her an enemy.

~

Speaking of **Hannah**...wow! She has a wonderful journey. She was loved by her husband and he took really good care of her. Still, Hannah had years of pain and anguish. But, she had great faith and trusted God. She promised God if He would give her a son, she would give that boy right back to Him. That took courage! God honored that courage and gave her five more children; three sons and two daughters. The son she gave back to God was named Samuel. He became an important prophet in Jewish history. It must have been wonderful as his mother to watch him grow up and serve the Lord in the way he did.

Hannah may have taken matters into her own hands slightly by 'bargaining' with God, but she left it up to Him to answer or not. She didn't take a short cut like Sarah and Rachel did. She asked God to answer her prayer and then promised, if He did, she would dedicate that son to the Lord's service. That's a beautiful, wonderful sacrifice. And she kept her word.

~

Elizabeth is another woman of amazing faith. She was a private, godly woman who reveled in the blessing God was giving her. She knew the baby she carried was set aside for the Lord's service. She kept the joy and the blessing to herself for as long as she could. Scripture tells us five months. For five months she stayed home and just enjoyed being pregnant. For five months, she communed with her heavenly Father and enjoyed the favor He had granted her.

I've often wondered if Elizabeth and Zacharias were still alive when their amazing son was beheaded by Herod. I hope they weren't. What heartache that would have been, to see your son killed in such a senseless fashion (Matthew 14:1-12).

Mary the mother of Jesus wasn't spared that pain. Mary was a pure young woman who approached the news she was the chosen virgin to bring the Messiah into the world with awe and wonder. She was obedient at every step of the way. How it must have ripped her heart out to watch her first born suffer on the cross. But oh, the joy of seeing Him resurrected on the third day! (John 19:25-27)

We know very little about Mary, Joseph and Jesus in his early years. We only know from scripture how He was conceived, the circumstances of His birth and a short story about him staying in the city and hanging out at the Temple after his parents left to go home to a different city. He was 'lost' for a number of days. When they finally found Him, they were mad and he was surprised. They talked about what happened and all is made well. That's it. That's all we know. (Luke 2:41-52)

We see more of Mary once Jesus started His ministry, but He's the main show. There are several scriptures that tell us Mary pondered things in her heart. She would hear things about her son and treasure them. Maybe not in the same way most mother's would, but maybe in a way to grasp this son of hers was fully God and fully man. That's a really big concept. He was her baby. He was her little boy. Her teenager. Her grown son. But He was never really 'hers' at all. He belongs to all of us who believe.

The wife of the Danite, mother of Samson doesn't even get a name in scripture. There's only one chapter dedicated to this story. It's in Judges 13. Verse 3 tells us the Angel of the Lord appeared to her. He doesn't tell her to not be afraid. Because of this, it would be logical to think she wasn't afraid. She's told even though she's barren, she's going to have a child. The Angel of the Lord gives her specific instructions about what she is to eat and drink and instructions for the baby. She is told this baby will begin to deliver Israel from the hands of the Philistines. Her response? Go tell the hubby what has transpired.

She seemed to just take it all in stride. This is what happened. This is what I was told. This is what I'm supposed to do and this is what we're supposed to do for the kid. The one that seemed confused is Manoah, the husband. It's like he didn't believe his wife. So he asked God to send the Angel of the Lord back so he could talk with him. God did. The angel of the Lord appeared again to the woman. She went and got Manoah. Manoah essentially asked what the baby was going to be when he grew up. The Nazarite vow was typically for a short time. The idea of the child being set apart for his entire life seemed to be a foreign idea to the couple. It's possible that had never happened before.

The Angel of the Lord repeated what He'd already said, but emphasizes the message was for his wife, because she needed to be a part of the vow for a time. One can almost hear her saying, "I told you so". Manoah offered to feed their visitor, not realizing just who he was talking to. He told Manoah to offer a sacrifice instead. Manoah did and the Lord ascended in the flame of the altar. Now they realized they were in the presence of God. Manoah was afraid they were going to die. But his wife, seemingly the practical one of the couple, explained if God wanted them dead, they'd be dead. And, He has a mission for us, so He's not going to kill us.

I like her. She didn't get scared. She was very direct and plain spoken. We don't even know how she felt about getting pregnant. She seems very stoic and matter of fact. She completed her mission and gave birth to Samson.

Lastly, there is **Leah**. Leah's journey is the most beautiful. It's kind of rotten, what her dad asked her to do. She started out with high hopes of winning over her new husband with babies. It just didn't work. Her heart was broken. Jacob never treated her with the honor and care the first wife and mother of so many children deserved. One can surmise she and her sister were at odds most of the time. But Leah's faith never wavered. She loved the Lord and found a way, in time, to be content in her situation. She came to a place of peace. She outlived her sister and was buried with Jacob in the family tomb. She may not have had honor from her husband throughout her life, but God saw to it she was honored in death by where she was buried. She didn't become bitter. She didn't take vengeance. She didn't take matters into her own hands. She just simply stayed the course with her eyes on God. That's a faith journey worth mimicking.

We've looked at so many examples of women; barren and fertile. So many different responses to difficult circumstances, unique family dynamics, special callings from God and cultural customs. I can imagine you see yourself in one or more of these journeys. I know I do. I see myself in the impatience of Sarah and Rachel. I see myself in the bargaining of Hannah and the attempt to manipulate circumstances by Rebekkah. I have had moments of faith-excellence in my journey. I've had moments of faith failures along the way too.

My hope and prayer is that you find some encouragement in the principles I've laid out in these pages regarding what God has to say on the empty womb. I pray you will be encouraged by the journeys of the women written about in this book. I pray that as you write your own story, live out your own journey, walk your own path, you will come to a place of peace and contentment, no matter how your story ends. No matter whether the answer is yes, no or wait. Whatever the answer, it's a really big deal to God, because *you* are a really big deal to God.

"Sing, barren woman, who has never had a baby. Fill the air with song, you who've never experienced childbirth! You're ending up with far more children than all those childbearing women. God says so! Clear lots of ground for your tents! Make your tents large. Spread out! Think big! Use plenty of rope, drive the tent pegs deep. You're going to need lots of elbow room for your growing family. You're going to take over whole nations; you're going to resettle abandoned cities. Don't be afraid – you're not going to come up short. You'll forget all about the humiliations of your youth, and the indignities of being a widow will fade from memory. For your Maker is your bridegroom, his name, God-of-the-Angel-Armies! Your Redeemer is the Holy of Israel, known as God of the whole earth. You were like an abandoned wife, devastated with grief, and God welcomed you back, Like a woman married young and then left, says your God.

Your Redeemer God says:

It's with lasting love that I'm tenderly caring for you" (Isaiah 54:1-7, 8b The Message).

A special message to the woman who has lost children – I can't imagine your pain. I know women who suffered miscarriages or had babies die in utero. I know women who have lost children who are infants, toddlers, early school age, teens, young adults and older adults. It's not supposed to be that way. There's something truly horrible and unnatural for a parent to bury a child.

I've struggled to figure out how to grieve the loss of something I never had. When I compare that struggle to the loss of a child, no matter what age or stage of life that child of yours was in, I'm overwhelmed at the magnitude of your grief. I'm so sorry for your pain. Please know God sees you. Know God hears your cries of pain and He knows the depth of your pain. You are loved.

A special message to the woman whose quiver is full – I'm happy for you! I am. And so are your friends who have a closed womb and empty arms. It's just hard sometimes, to hear the cries of your baby and the laughter of your children. Be compassionate. Don't pity her though. That makes it worse. She doesn't need your pity. She needs your listening ear, your presence and your prayers. Bring comfort to her by involving her in your life and including her in your activities…with and without your children present.

Be sensitive with your questions. Some women don't mind talking about it. Others find it too painful. It's okay to ask questions. "Do you have children?" Is a safe question. If the answer is no, a good follow up would be "Did you (or do you) want children?" I've found out not every woman does! If the answer is 'Yes,' and she doesn't volunteer anymore, just ask, "Is it something you feel comfortable talking about?"

Compassion and comfort go a long way when offered with kindness and consideration.

A special message to the woman who hasn't been rescued by Jesus. I can't imagine going through all of this without the Lord loving me, leading me, growing me, guiding me, pursuing me, providing for me and protecting me. I'm a mess. I can be mean and unkind. I'm often selfish and thoughtless and I don't deserve the grace and love He extends to me hour by hour and day by day.

Romans 3:23 tells us we all have faults and bad behaviors that cause us to be apart from God. The consequence of that is an eternity without ever knowing Him. Those who don't look to Jesus to rescue them from that separation will never be united with God. They will spend eternity in a very lonely, dark place of suffering. That's the bad news.

The good news is while we were still knee deep in the muck and mire of our mess, God made a way for us to be rescued. But God demonstrates His own love toward us, in that while we were yet sinners, Christ died for us (Romans 5:8).

Jesus became the sacrifice needed to cover your sin and mine, once and for all.

But there's more to it than just Jesus dying a horrible, ugly and painful death on the cross for you and me. He overcame death and was resurrected on the third day after His burial! He's alive my friend!

It's hard to imagine the God who created the universe wants a relationship with you. He does. There's nothing you can do to earn His love and grace. It's a gift to you. In fact, He even gives you the faith to believe!

Ephesians 2 says this. Saving is all his idea, and all his work. All we do is trust him enough to let him do it. It's God's gift from start to finish (Ephesians 2:7).

Rescue by Jesus is right there, at your fingertips for the taking. But you just must receive it. If you confess with your mouth Jesus as Lord and believe in your heart that God raised Him from the dead, you will be saved (Romans 10:9).

Once you've done that, you're a new creature in Christ and an adopted child of the Most High God.

Therefore, if anyone is in Christ, he is a new creature; the old things passed away; behold, new things have come (2 Corinthians 5:17)

But as many as received Him, to them He gave the right to become children of God, even to those who believe in His name (John 1:12).[10]

He has already chosen you. He already loves YOU. Will you choose Him today?

10 All scripture on pages 93-94 are from The Message version

Discussion Questions
for small group or individual study

Chapter 1 Questions

Read Psalm 127. Is your quiver full or empty?

What word best describes where you are in your quest to become a mother?

The Hebrew word for ashamed is *buwah*. It means to be disappointed, to be delayed, to become dry. Have you ever felt a sense of shame in your infertility journey? Explain.

Have you felt your barrenness was punishment or a consequence for past sin(s)? Explain.

Are you blessed if you don't have children? How and in what ways?

The Hebrew word for reward is *sakar*. It means payment of contract, wages, compensation or benefit. How does this contractual nature of having children in Old Testament times make you feel? What was the purpose?

Have you considered barrenness may be a consequence of the original sin and living in a fallen world? If that's the case, how does that idea jive with scripture saying God alone opens and closes wombs?

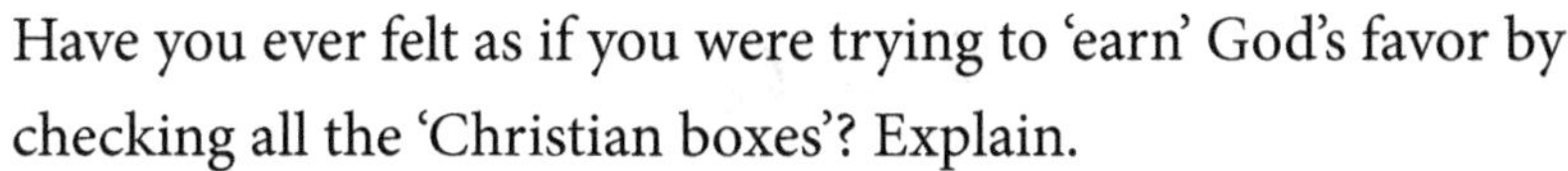

Have you ever felt as if you were trying to 'earn' God's favor by checking all the 'Christian boxes'? Explain.

In Psalms 127:3, the King James Version says, 'children are an heritage of the Lord'. Your Bible may say 'gift'. The Hebrew word for heritage is *nachel*. It means to inherit something like an heirloom. What does this tell you about God's view of children?

Read Luke 1:26-38. How would you describe Mary's reaction to Gabriel's announcement?

The Hebrew Word for build is *banah*. It means to obtain children and have many descendants. How have you labored in vain in your infertility journey?

Chapter 2 Questions

Read Matthew 9:20-22, Mark 5: 25-34 and Luke 8: 43-48. How do you relate to the woman with the blood issue?

What kind of emotional, psychological and physical toll do you think her issue took on her?

What impact do you think Jesus calling her daughter had on her weary, hurt heart?

Share some of the tests and procedures you've endured in your infertility journey. What's your 'back story'?

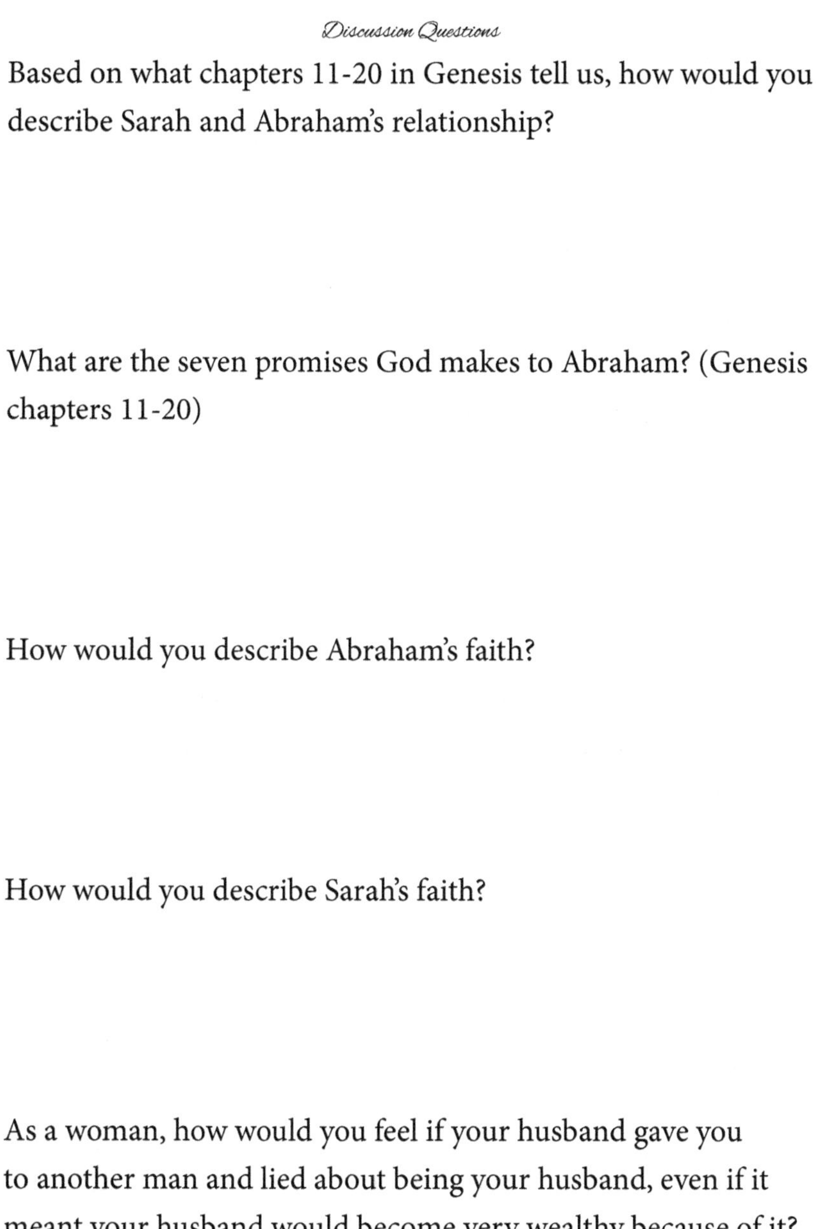

Based on what chapters 11-20 in Genesis tell us, how would you describe Sarah and Abraham's relationship?

What are the seven promises God makes to Abraham? (Genesis chapters 11-20)

How would you describe Abraham's faith?

How would you describe Sarah's faith?

As a woman, how would you feel if your husband gave you to another man and lied about being your husband, even if it meant your husband would become very wealthy because of it?

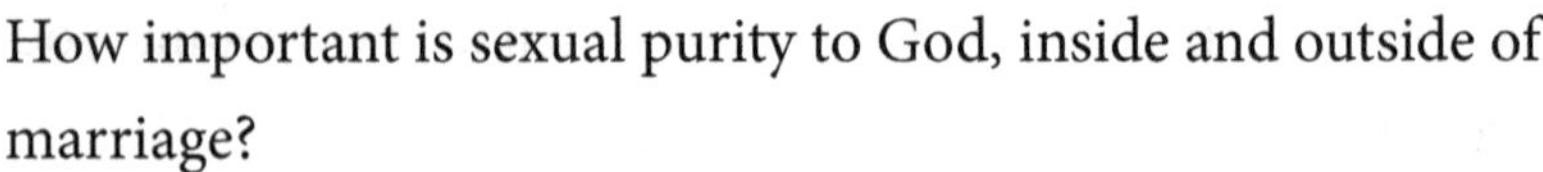
How important is sexual purity to God, inside and outside of marriage?

God protected Sarah, Abraham and Abimelech. How has God protected you in general and specifically in your infertility journey?

One of the last things we see in this section of scripture (Gen 20:17-18 specifically) is Abraham prayed. He asked for healing of Abimelech, his wife and his maids. God heard. God healed. What does it mean to you that God heard, and answered, Abraham's prayers despite his screw up and lack of faith?

Do you trust God's sovereignty? How do you live that out?

Do you believe God always has your best at heart, even if it's different from what you want? Explain.

If your desire for a child never comes to pass, will you still trust God? Love God? Worship God? With your whole heart and with sincerity?

Chapter 3 Questions

What influence may Abraham have had on his grandson, Jacob the deceiver?

Why do you think Jacob was attracted to Rachel over Leah? (Gen 29-30)

The Hebrew word for 'tender-eyed' is *rak*. Scripture says this about Leah in Genesis 29:17. *Rak* means soft-hearted or tender-hearted, not that she couldn't see. With a sweet disposition like that, why do you think Leah went along with Laban's deception to marry Jacob instead of Rachel?

Leah was unloved and having babies. Rachel was loved, but there were no babies. Leah says in Gen 29:32, when Ruben was born, that the Lord had seen her affliction. The Hebrew word for affliction is *oiny*. It means depression, misery and trouble. Based on this statement, how do you think things were going between the sisters?

Leah believed God saw her affliction when Ruben was born. The Hebrew word for saw is *raah* and means consider, take heed and be near. At the birth of Simeon, Leah says in Gen 29:33, the Lord has heard I'm unloved. The Hebrew word for heard is *shama*. It means to give ear or attentively listen. Leah felt God saw her and heard her. Do you feel God hears you and sees you?

Leah was still hoping for love from Jacob when baby Levi came along. Gen 29:34 she says, "Now this time my husband will become attached to me." The Hebrew word for attached is *lavah* and means to unite, abide with and cleave. Leah's greatest desire was for Jacob to love her. Yet that desire was not granted, as far as we know from scripture. What is your greatest desire? How will you feel if that desire is filled?

When baby Judah was born, Leah simply said she would praise the Lord. (Gen 29:35). What changed?

How was Rachel's attitude toward Jacob different than Leah? What do you think about her blaming Jacob for not getting her pregnant? Why do you think she would say that to him? Have you taken steps in your life to attempt to control the uncontrollable?

God finally remembered Rachel and opened her womb. (Gen 30:22) Rachel got the desire of her heart, but Leah didn't, as far as we know from scripture. Why does such a loving God answer some prayers, but says 'no' to others? How does this make you feel? What does this tell you about God?

God answered another prayer for Rachel that cost her her life. (Gen 35:16-20) Do you think sometimes God gives us what we want, even when it's not the best thing for us? Can you think of some examples from scripture?

How do you think the relationship between Leah and Jacob changed once Rachel died? Do you think she finally got the place of honor that was rightfully hers as his first wife and the mother of so many of his sons?

Chapter 4 Questions

Read 1 Samuel 1:1-28. Do you relate to Hannah? Have you poured out your grief and disappointment to the Lord? Have you 'bargained' with Him?

The King James version says Peninnah 'provoked her sore' in her torment of Hannah. She vexed her and caused her to have a great deal of sorrow. Is there an antagonist in your life who tries to make you feel 'less' because your quiver is empty? How do you deal with it?

Do you have an encourager in your corner like Elkanah was to Hannah?

How do you think Hannah felt leaving her little boy Samuel in the hands of Eli the priest to raise? Could you do that, even if you promised God?

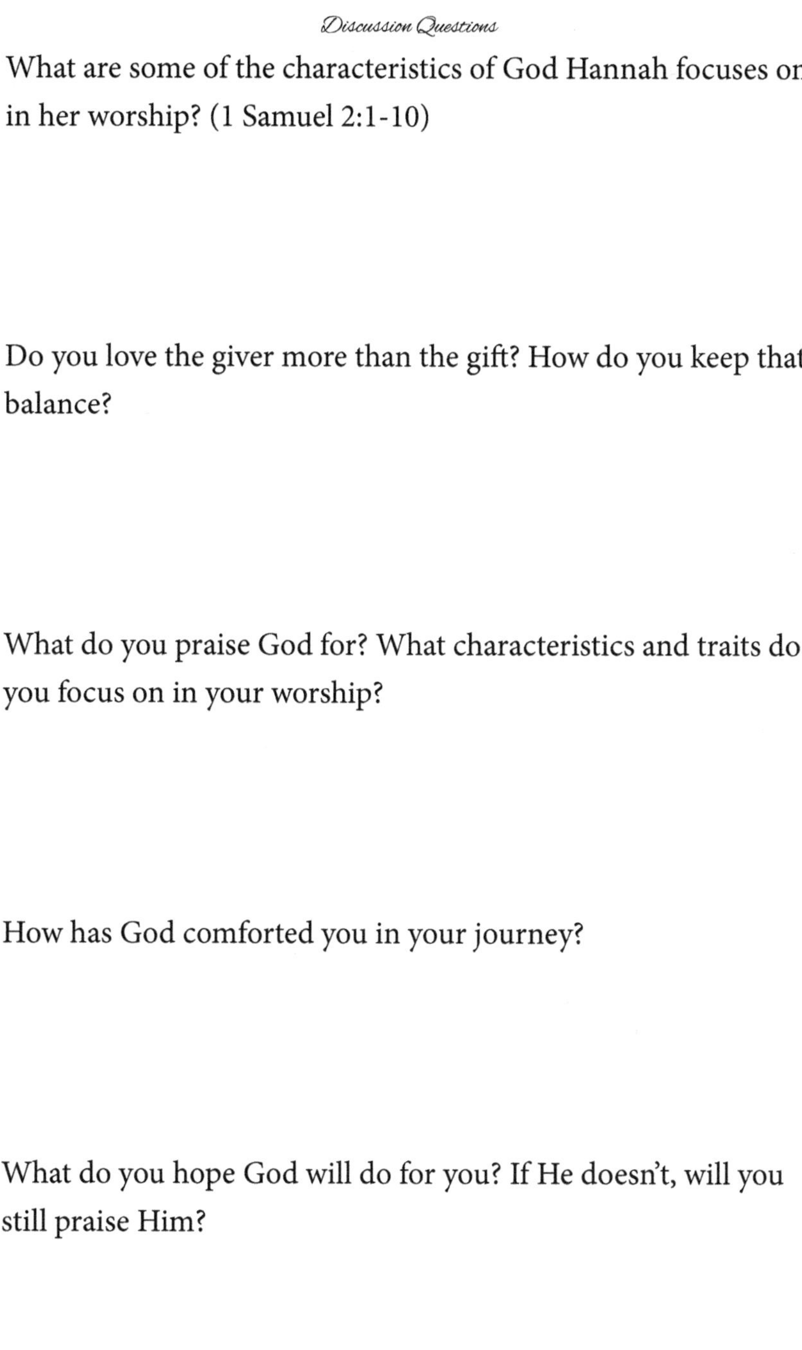

What are some of the characteristics of God Hannah focuses on in her worship? (1 Samuel 2:1-10)

Do you love the giver more than the gift? How do you keep that balance?

What do you praise God for? What characteristics and traits do you focus on in your worship?

How has God comforted you in your journey?

What do you hope God will do for you? If He doesn't, will you still praise Him?

Who else is praying for you? Who is your Abraham, Isaac or Zacharias?

Chapter 5 Questions

Read Luke chapter 1.

Luke 1:6 tells us Elizabeth and Zacharias were blameless in the eyes of God. The Greek word for blameless is *amemptos*. It means irreproachable and faultless. Because they kept God's commandments, precepts, ordinances and requirements according to Jewish Law, this could be said of them. What would this look like today, since we're in Christ and not under Jewish Law?

How would you react if the Angel Gabriel appeared to you? Have you ever heard God speak audibly? How do you know God's voice?

What are the four things Gabe says about Baby John? Why are these significant?

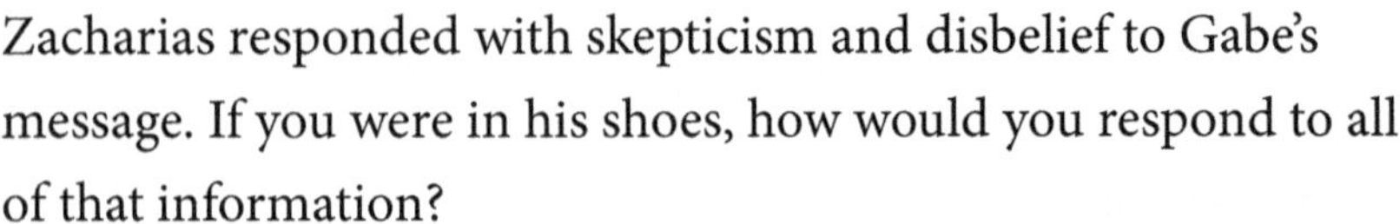

Zacharias responded with skepticism and disbelief to Gabe's message. If you were in his shoes, how would you respond to all of that information?

How was Mary's response to Gabe's message different than Zacharias?

Why do you think Elizabeth stayed in seclusion for 5 months, not sharing her amazing news?

There are three examples in this chapter of God doing the impossible; two old women getting pregnant, (Sarah and Elizabeth) generations apart, and a virgin getting pregnant. Do you believe nothing is impossible with God? Why or why not?

Do you trust God's timing to be perfect – never early, never late – even though it may feel that way? Why or why not?

Chapter 6 Questions

Look again at Proverbs 13:12a, Psalm 31:24, 33:18,22, 42:5 and 43:5. Do you have hope or are you in despair? Is your hope in the Lord? Are you focused on Him?

If your quiver is empty, have you grieved that loss? Why or why not?

If you are childless, have you become bitter? What affect is that having on you, your relationships with others and your relationship with God?

List the examples of the many times in scripture the point is made that a woman (or women) was barren. Why was that important? What does this tell you about what God thinks about infertility?

What was the purpose in Sarah's womb being closed? What was the purpose in Elizabeth's womb being closed?

What was the purpose in Sarah's womb being opened? What was the purpose in Elizabeth's womb being opened? Hannah? Rachel and Leah? The wife of the Danite? (Judges 13)

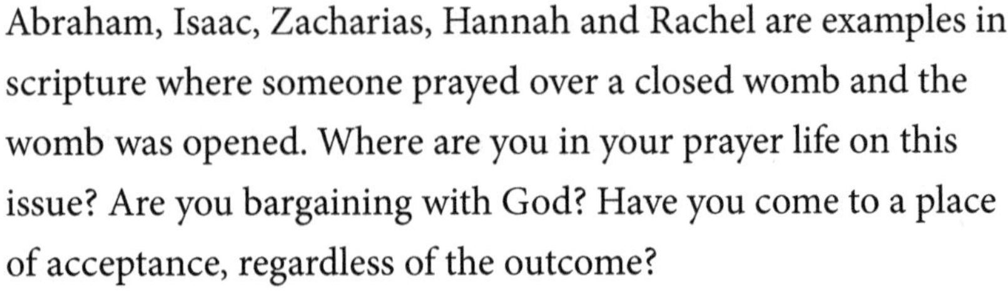

Abraham, Isaac, Zacharias, Hannah and Rachel are examples in scripture where someone prayed over a closed womb and the womb was opened. Where are you in your prayer life on this issue? Are you bargaining with God? Have you come to a place of acceptance, regardless of the outcome?

There are three ways God answers prayer; yes, no and wait. Where are you in your prayer journey regarding infertility? Have you received a definite 'yes, no or wait'?

Do you believe the closed womb is a really big deal to God? Why or why not?

Chapter 7 Questions

There is one other woman who had an interesting journey not discussed within the pages of this book. Michal. Let's take a look at her journey. Read 1 Samuel 14:49, 18:17-29, 19:11-17, 25:44, 2 Samuel 3:12-16, and 2 Samuel Chapter 6.

Describe Michal's journey with David. Why did Saul give her away to Paltiel? Why do you think Michal never had children? What changed for her towards David? What changed for David towards Michal?

Which woman's journey from scripture do you most relate to? Why?

Which principle talked about in the pages of this book resonates the most with you? Why?

Read Isaiah 54. What does this passage mean to you? How does it encourage you?

Describe your journey – all of it. The tests. The pain – physical and emotional. The praying, the grieving. Put it all down. God sees. God hears. God knows your pain.

About the Author

Audrey Wyatt Shrive began her infertility journey in her late twenties. For nearly fifteen years she struggled to conceive. Yearning to understand what God had to say on the matter, Audrey sought truth from the best source she knew, The Bible. She discovered God has a great deal to say on of barrenness and the empty womb. A twenty year student on the subject, Audrey pens her discoveries in the pages of this book, with the hope of encouraging other women with similar challenges.

Audrey is a Christian living speaker, who gets great joy from speaking at women's events and bringing God's word on this topic and many others. Audrey is a story teller and realizes when she writes and speaks, she's using the talents God has given her. She can feel His pleasure in those moments!

Originally from South Western South Dakota, Audrey and her husband Steve currently reside in Colorado Springs, Colorado where they love and raise Siberian Huskies. They are active in their church and host a weekly Bible study in their home. They are avid football fans, although they don't agree on teams at all. Audrey enjoys gardening, canning and reading when she's not writing. She plays the alto saxophone in a community band.

Audrey's first book, *This is from Me*, a memoir about her divorce and how God provided for her and protected her through that journey is available on Amazon. You can connect with Audrey on her website, thisisfromme.com or on her Facebook Page, This is from Me.

www.ingramcontent.com/pod-product-compliance
Lightning Source LLC
Chambersburg PA
CBHW060815050426
42449CB00008B/1676
* 9 7 8 1 7 3 6 2 7 2 0 3 9 *